The Dark Fantastic
12 Short Screenplays

by
Lee McQueen

McQueen♛Press

Chicago, IL

Published by McQueen Press
http://mcqueenpress.wordpress.com

About the Author
Lee McQueen's roots stretch deep into the world of writing, research, analysis, and public affairs. With a Master of Library Science from SUNY-Buffalo, a Bachelor of Arts from Xavier University of Louisiana and graduate coursework in public affairs at the University of Texas, she has been a librarian, a bookstore owner, and a writer-for-hire of websites, press releases, newsletter articles, and encyclopedia entries. She also writes short stories, poems, novels, and screenplays, creates original watercolor greeting cards, and self-publishes.

"Stephanie" based upon the short story "The Confessions of the Dreamers" by Lee McQueen (*Imaginarium*, McQueen Press, 2006).

"The Lovebirds" based upon the short story "The Lovebirds" by Lee McQueen (*Imaginarium*, McQueen Press, 2006).

"Davey in the Lying Time" based upon the 1st Edition screenplay *The Angel and the Lion* by Lee McQueen (McQueen Press, 2005) registered with the Library of Congress as *The Angel and the Lion*, alternative title *SUDAN: The Lion of Truth*. First edition of *The Angel and the Lion* screenplay registered with the Writers Guild of America, west, as *SUDAN* (2005). "The Angel and the Lion" short story by Lee McQueen first published in *Imaginarium* (McQueen Press, 2006). Second edition of *The Angel and the Lion* republished under the title *SUDAN: The Lion of Truth* (McQueen Press, 2011).

"Pretty Diamonds and Rubies" based upon the novel *Kenzi* by Lee McQueen (McQueen Press, 2006).

"Celara Electric" based upon the novel *Celara Sun* by Lee McQueen (McQueen Press, 2010).

"King of the City" based upon the novel *Windrunner* by Lee McQueen (McQueen Press, 2012).

"Johnnie Ganjaweed" based upon the short story "The Reversal" by Lee McQueen (*Imaginarium*, McQueen Press, 2006).

"Sunday" based upon the short story "Children of the Golden Ra" by Lee McQueen (*Imaginarium*, McQueen Press, 2006).

"Roads to Mexico" based upon the short story "Welcome to Aztlan!" by Lee McQueen (*Imaginarium*, McQueen Press, 2006).

Cover design, interior design, and typesetting by Lee McQueen.

Logo registered mark of McQueen Press.

ISBN 978-0-9798515-5-1

Publisher's Catalog-in-Publication

McQueen, Lee
The Dark Fantastic: Twelve Short Screenplays/ Lee McQueen
p. cm.
ISBN
  1. Adventure fiction
  2. Science fiction
  3. Horror fiction
  4. Motion picture plays.
I. Title

Works by Lee McQueen

Short Story Collection
Imaginarium

Poetry
Things I Forgot to Tell You

Novels
Kenzi

Celara Sun

Windrunner

Screenplays
Kindred

SUDAN: The Lion of Truth

Non-Fictions
Writer in the Library! 41 Writers Reveal How They Use
Libraries to Develop Their Skill, Craft & Careers

Road Romance: Tales From the Book Tour

For the Believers:
Octavia Butler, Isaac Asimov, Edgar Allen Poe,
Frida Kahlo, Giorgio de Chirico,
Samuel Barber, and Miles Davis

Table of Contents

Introduction

When did I start writing, I'm frequently asked. The answer is, once I learned how to write, I never stopped. I've been writing for as long as I can remember.

In fact, few episodes in life cause me more embarrassment than grade school photographs and grade school poems and stories that I wrote for Teacher that I've had shown to me by my family amid jolly laughter.

But I didn't claim myself as a writer until people began to request my work, and then paid me for it. My writing career began with book and movie reviews, public affairs essays, encyclopedia entries, newsletter articles, and then work-for-hire website content and press releases. In other words, non-fiction. I self-published two full-length non-fictions, three novels, a short story collection, and a book of poetry.

Five of the twelve screenplays in *The Dark Fantastic* originated as short stories in the *Imaginarium* collection, self-published in 2006. Those short stories were written for easy and optimistic conversion to screenplay format. My goal during the screenplay adaptations was to see if I could make improvements. Having grown as a writer in the seven years since *Imaginarium's* publication, I found improvements to each story, though most changes were necessary anyway to conform to established industry screenplay format, to keep track of page count, to accelerate the action, to increase the tension, and to tighten the suspense.

"Stephanie" is a modern-day *Fall of the House of Usher* that describes the ways in which ties that bind also smother to death. Adapted from *Imaginarium's* "The Confessions of the Dreamers," this screenplay narrates the self-destruction of a middle class family somewhere in North America. The teenage female protagonist desires to discover the solution to her family's secrets before she becomes another victim.

"The Lovebirds" is a horror story from *Imaginarium* that reveals the unspeakable—that not only women got raped during the seventeenth-century slave trade. The teenage male protagonist desires to reclaim his manhood and his freedom. In a tale so loathsome that it has never been told until now, a sinister and systematic method for breaking a man, degrading a man, destroying a man, driving a man to insanity and murder chills not because it likely happened many times in history, but also chills because it happens today in the modern North American prison system.

"Davey in the Lying Time" is a suspense drama that began as a feature-length action-adventure screenplay—*The Angel and the Lion*—published in 2006 to stand alone. A former gang member joins a Christian mission to free trafficked women, but is instead captured herself. That screenplay metamorphosed into "The Angel and the Lion" short story published in

Imaginarium. The full-length screenplay was then republished as *SUDAN:The Lion of Truth* in 2011. This latest iteration moves the story's setting from the African desert to where it really belongs, the border regions of Texas and Mexico where women disappear with no answers provided to no questions asked.

"Pretty Diamonds and Rubies" is based upon the novel *Kenzi* by Lee McQueen (McQueen Press, 2006). An alcoholic, rage-filled woman drives herself into a wall.

"You Have to Pay the Cost to be the Boss" is an original story that reveals the hard path to success and the price paid to reach that end goal. Similar in tone to the "Picture of Dorian Gray," the male protagonist must answer the question, "Was the ride to the top worth the cost?"

Celara Sun by Lee McQueen (McQueen Press, 2010) inspires "Celara Electric," a three-person suspense that occurs in a car and then a bridge on an icy road in the blackest hours of early morning when there are no witnesses. The female protagonist must decide whether or not to join the dark side of business intelligence.

"King of the City" is another three-person suspense based upon the novel *Windrunner* by Lee McQueen (McQueen Press, 2012). In this battle of wills, the female protagonist tries to survive a confrontation with two powerful political figures.

"Faraway, Iowa" is an original short screenplay without dialogue that explores the future social landscape of this Midwestern state. A woman burdened by an unintended pregnancy struggles to save herself from the consequences of the community's harsh judgment of her choice.

"Deep in the Woods" is another original short screenplay that intrudes on the debate between a mother and father who are forced into a corner. In this biblically-based futuristic horror, the worst aspects of human nature surface to consume hearth and home.

On the lighter side, "Johnnie Ganjaweed" is a road adventure adapted from *Imaginarium's* "The Reversal" that describes how one spirited young woman, an ex-offender and parole violator, stops the Drug War. Johnny Appleseed comes to modern life in a tale of whimsy that comments on one of the most destructive national public policies in North America.

"Sunday" is a slick boardroom drama where everyone looks cool, walks cool, and talks cool. Based upon "Children of the Golden Ra" from *Imaginarium,* a restless crime lord desires to move way ahead of the game. So he shows his colleagues entrenched in conventional criminal enterprises precisely how to control the solar energy industry. Build it and they will come. But if you build it and destroy all others, they will come running!

"Roads to Mexico" is a speculation on a migration of North Americans to Mexico whose army greets U.S. citizens, not with open arms, but with irritated suspicion. Based upon the original story, "Welcome to Aztlan!" from

Imaginarium, The female protagonist must talk her way across the border, decide her political loyalties, improve her conversational Spanish, and fall in love. Good times.

A painter paints. A singer sings. A dancer dances. An actor acts. A writer writes.

Through bureaucracy, travel, family, work, recession, and life in general; a writer will always write.

I thank the reader for reading!

Lee McQueen
Chicago, IL
2013

McQueen♟Press

Screenplay 1

Stephanie

CAST OF CHARACTERS

Roy Brazil - African-American, male, mid-40s

Susan Brazil - African-American, female, 42

Marietta Brazil - African-American, female, 17

Stephanie Madison - African-American, female, 42

Grandma Madison (voice only) - female, mid-60s

News Reader (voice only)

Minister (voice only)

Veterinarian (voice only)

Police Officer (voice only)

Nurse (voice only)

Doctor (voice only)

Male Student (voice only) - 16 to 18
Female Student (voice only) - 16 to 18

TIME
Present day.

FADE IN

INT. SUSAN'S HOUSE:SUSAN'S BEDROOM - DAY

SUSAN looks into the mirror, expressionless. She puts on makeup.

INT. ROY'S CONDO:MARIETTA'S ROOM - DAY

ROY pauses in the doorway to his daughter's room.

> ROY
> Marietta, we have to cut the
> weekend short. Stephanie died
> this morning.

MARIETTA looks up from her homework.

> MARIETTA
> Aunt Stephanie? But she's only
> forty-two, just like Mom.

INT. SUSAN'S HOUSE:SUSAN'S BEDROOM - DAY

Susan smooths her hair back into a tight bun.

INT. ROY'S CONDO:MARIETTA'S ROOM - DAY

> MARIETTA
> How did she die?

                    ROY
          Susan's already on her way to
          pick you up. It's probably
          better that you hear it from
          her.

INT. SUSAN'S HOUSE:HALLWAY - DAY

Susan picks up car keys.

INT. ROY'S CONDO - DAY

                    ROY
          Marietta, she... (hesitates)
          Well, the funny thing is,
          Stephanie sent you something
          care of me. It arrived this
          morning. I opened the box to
          make sure it was okay. But
          this (Roy hands her a thick
          book) is still in the
          wrapper.

                    MARIETTA
          I didn't think Stephanie was
          religious. None of us have
          been to church since Grandma
          died last year.

                    ROY
          There's a lot about Stephanie
          that no one ever knew and
          never will.

Roy hugs Marietta.

                    ROY
          Go ahead and get packed,
          sweetheart. Don't answer your
          phone or go online, Okay?

INT. SUSAN'S CAR - DAY

Susan listens to news of Stephanie's death on the car
radio.

INT. ROY'S CONDO - DAY

Marietta stands at the top of the stairs eavesdropping.

                    ROY (pleading)
          Susan, I'm… I'm sorry.

A long silence.

                    SUSAN (icy)
          Really. Are you.

                    ROY
          It… doesn't have to be like
          this.

                    SUSAN
          But it *is* like this. You made
          sure of that. Didn't you?

                    MARIETTA (whispers)
          Jeez, Dad. Don't cry again.

Marietta slings her backpack over her shoulders and goes
downstairs.

INT. SUSAN'S CAR - DAY

Radio's off.

                    MARIETTA
          Mom, what happened to Aunt
          Stephanie?

                    SUSAN (abruptly)
          She was shot down by police.

                    MARIETTA
          What?

Susan sighs and smooths her hair in the rear-view mirror.

                    SUSAN
          Marietta, you remember that I
          told   you   Stephanie   was
          unstable? And that you should
          stay away from her?

                    MARIETTA
          Yes. And I did. I stayed away
          like you told me.

                    SUSAN
          Sometimes, when you walk a
          tightrope, you make it to the
          other side. Other times, you
          don't. You fall off.

Susan shoots Marietta a glance.

                    SUSAN
          Stephanie made it across many
          times. As a matter of fact,
          she got real good at it. But
          she crossed one time too many.

Marietta looks at Susan's hands as she turns the steering
wheel.

                    MARIETTA
          Why did they shoot her?

                    SUSAN
          She wanted them to shoot her.

Susan's fingers tighten to a bloodless white.

                    SUSAN
          It's all over the radio.

Marietta reaches to switch the radio on.

Susan blocks her hand.

                    SUSAN
          No.

Marietta reaches in her backpack for her cell phone.

                    SUSAN
          Not now. Look, it's all over
          television too. That's why I
          came to get you as soon as I
          could so you'd be ready for
          all the...

Susan shakes her head and looks away.

               SUSAN
Marietta, just don't answer
your phone tonight. Okay?
Don't answer any emails. Don't
go online or watch t.v. Do
that for me?

Marietta nods.

INT. SUSAN'S HOUSE:MARIETTA'S ROOM - NIGHT

Marietta overhears press inquiries on the answering
machine in the hallway and Susan's voice fielding more
calls on her cell phone.

INT. SUSAN'S HOUSE:KITCHEN - NIGHT

Marietta goes downstairs to heat leftovers in the
microwave.

INT. SUSAN'S HOUSE:LIVING ROOM - NIGHT

A NEWS READER discusses Stephanie's death on television.

               NEWS READER (voice)
The deceased, forty-two-year-
old Stephanie Madison...

               SUSAN (voice)
…threatened me just last
week...

               NEWS READER (voice)
...purchased the thirty-eight
special legally…

                    SUSAN (voice)
          …Something just told me it…

                    NEWS READER (voice)
          …family members that Stephanie
          Madison had a history of other
          incidences   of   intimidation
          and...

                    SUSAN (voice)
          … the last time I would see
          her alive...

                    NEWS READER (voice)
          terrorism, local police issued
          a warrant for her arrest...

Marietta creeps closer to the kitchen door.

                    SUSAN
          …business   card   from   an
          abortion doctor in her wallet.
          I don't know. With Stephanie,
          who ever does...

Marietta hears Susan sigh loudly close to the kitchen
door.

INT. SUSAN'S HOUSE:LIVING ROOM - NIGHT

                    SUSAN
          I was so afraid for Marietta.

INT. SUSAN'S HOUSE:MARIETTA'S ROOM - NIGHT

Marietta races upstairs and closes her bedroom door.

She finds an online video titled, Stephanie Madison's Last
Stand. In a slow-motion ballet of bullets set to *Adagio
for Strings*, STEPHANIE'S wild hair swirls in the wind. Her
mouth screams a black hole. She hits the hood of her car
and drops the gun. Blood sprays.

The comment section underneath the video is celebratory,
awarding points for music score, special effects, and
sound editing.

Marietta cries and deletes emails and voice mails.

INT. SUSAN'S HOUSE:MARIETTA'S ROOM - DAY

Marietta peels the plastic from the Bible,

                MARIETTA (surprised)
          She used a blow-dryer.

EXT. CEMETARY - DAY

Marietta stands graveside between Roy and Susan holding
the Bible.

                MINISTER (voice)
          If only we could understand
          the reasons for Stephanie
          Madison's torment, and prevent
          others from sharing her
          fate...

Everyone except Susan, Roy, and Marietta leaves.

                    SUSAN
          Marietta, you understand why
          we couldn't announce the time
          and place to anyone? We don't
          need to deal with chaos right
          now.

Marietta nods.

                    SUSAN
          Thank God the police are here
          to keep the vultures at bay.

Marietta aims a glance at the police without reply.

                    SUSAN
          Some of the family and our
          friends will drop things off
          at the house. But they're not
          gonna stay. It's all... just
          too much right now.

                    ROY
          I need to make a stop first.
          I'll meet you guys at the
          house.

Susan provides Roy with a cool glance and no reply.

INT. SUSAN'S HOME:KITCHEN - NIGHT

Marietta puts away containers of food.

INT. SUSAN'S HOUSE:LIVING ROOM - NIGHT

Susan straightens the living room with focused obsession.

The doorbell rings and Susan greets Roy in the doorway.

> SUSAN
> You should have asked me
> first.

> ROY
> I probably should have, but I
> wanted Marietta to at least
> have a chance to see him.

INT. SUSAN'S HOUSE:KITCHEN - NIGHT

Marietta hears Susan hiss something to Roy who doesn't
back down.

> SUSAN (exasperated)
> Marietta!

INT. SUSAN'S HOUSE:LIVING ROOM - NIGHT

The fluffy, golden dog yips and barks.

> MARIETTA (laughing)
> Oh, he's beautiful. He's so
> friendly.

Susan makes an impatient sound that Roy quickly covers.

> ROY
> He's all yours, Marietta. You
> get to name him.

> MARIETTA
> How about Jesse?

                    SUSAN
          Why are you naming him that?

                    ROY
          Jesse Brazil.

                    MARIETTA
          Because I miss Grandpa.

Susan frowns. Roy's meets Susan's gaze.

                    ROY
          Sounds good to me.

                    SUSAN
          Fine. Marietta, this dog is
          your responsibility. You're
          going to feed him and walk
          him. (frowns) And he sleeps
          outside.

                    MARIETTA
          Mom.

                    SUSAN
          Marietta, I mean it.

                    MARIETTA
          Why can't he sleep in my
          room?

Marietta looks at her father who looks away like *don't
push it, kid.*

                    SUSAN
          We don't know what he's
          carrying.

                    ROY (loudly)
          He has a clean bill of health
          from the vet.

                    SUSAN (dubious)
          If you say so.

                    ROY
          Susan, you're running out of
          excuses. He's fine.

                    SUSAN (screams)
          I said alright!

Jesse barks at Susan.

                    SUSAN
          Just remember the rules,
          Marietta.

EXT. SUSAN'S HOUSE:BACKYARD - DAY

Marietta sets up Jesse's backyard home with food and
supplies while Jesse runs around.

Susan calls to Marietta from the patio door.

                    SUSAN
          Marietta? Homework. Now.

INT. SUSAN'S HOUSE:MARIETTA'S ROOM - NIGHT

Marietta looks over her shoulder, then shoves Jesse into
her room.

Marietta taps on her laptop.

Jesse knocks the Bible off her nightstand.

The Bible lays open on the floor. Stuck between the pages are typewritten sheets of white paper, cut exactly to tuck into the spine without sticking out. Marietta pulls out a sheet and reads it.

> STEPHANIE (voiceover)
> She's doing it again. The only
> way Mama could have known was
> her.

Marietta slams the Bible shut.

After a moment of thought, she digs out the tablet that holds the video of the family's July 4th celebration in the Brazil backyard.

Stephanie, disheveled and confused, enters the backyard.

Voices off-camera hiss "Stephanie!" and "She's here!"

Marietta stops the video.

Later that night, while Marietta dreams, she hears...

> STEPHANIE (voice)
> My baby!

Marietta jerks awake, terrified, alone in her room.

The moon is full but hazy from a cover of clouds.

In the backyard, Jesse barks angrily.

INT. SUSAN'S HOUSE:KITCHEN - NIGHT

Marietta hurries downstairs. She hears, "Eeeyowrrrr!"

              MARIETTA
    Is that a cat?

Marietta shushes Jesse from the patio door and goes back
to bed.

INT. SUSAN'S HOUSE:BACKYARD - DAY

Susan shoves Jesse's nose away and clips dead leaves off
hedges with sharp, cold precision.

A NEIGHBOR speaks over the hedge.

              NEIGHBOR (voice)
    Poor kitty. I found it when I
    turned off my sprinklers.
    Buried it so it wouldn't draw
    rodents.

              SUSAN
    Disgusting. People are so
    irresponsible with their
    animals.

The neighbor nods agreement and smiles at Jesse's wild
barking.

Susan turns and marches away, offended.

INT. SUSAN'S HOUSE:KITCHEN - DAY

On her tablet, Marietta watches another video of Stephanie
standing motionless across the street from Marietta's high
school.

                    MALE STUDENT (voice)
          There's   that   homeless   lady
          again.   She's   talking   to
          herself.

Marietta quickly switches off her tablet and spreads honey
on toast as Susan shuts the patio door in Jesse's face and
locks it.

                    SUSAN
          Are you wondering why Jesse's
          in the backyard instead of
          your room where he wasn't
          supposed to be?

                    MARIETTA (looks down)
          No.

                    SUSAN
          Don't let it happen again.

Marietta nods, shame-faced.

                    MARIETTA
          Mom, I was just thinking about
          Stephanie again.

Susan washes her hands obsessively at the kitchen sink.

                    SUSAN
You know you can always talk
to me, Marietta. I'm your
mother.

                    MARIETTA
When do you think they'll
stop showing the video of the
police shooting her?

                    SUSAN
Have people been asking you
about Stephanie?

                    MARIETTA
Not anymore. I just don't
answer and they stop asking.

                    SUSAN (nods)
Good. The next big fire or
three-mile pile up should do
it. Whenever the police are
around, that's when the
cameras come out. Blood
money.

                    MARIETTA
Some people seem really upset
with the police for shooting
her.

Susan sighs, finishes with her hands and sits down.

                    SUSAN
          They want action against the
          police department. But I
          already let them and the
          police know that our family
          isn't interested in scandal.
          It's over. Like I said,
          Stephanie wanted to die.

                    MARIETTA
          Why do you keep saying that?

                    SUSAN (exasperated)
          It was suicide by cop,
          Marietta. It wasn't enough for
          her to...

Susan doesn't finish.

                    MARIETTA
          Mom, do you miss Aunt
          Stephanie?

                    SUSAN
          Yes. Yes, I... miss her.
          Despite all the strange
          behavior and the negativity,
          she was my sister.

                    MARIETTA
          When was the last time you saw
          her before she died?

Susan fiddles with the salt and pepper shakers.

                    SUSAN
          I ... months ago.

Marietta remembers Susan on the phone (voiceover)
...threatened me last week...

> SUSAN
> She fell into a bad crowd. So-
> called revolutionaries.
> Drinking. Probably drugs.
> Different men.

Susan shakes her head in sorrow.

> SUSAN
> She had a destructive
> personality. I didn't want
> any of that in my house or
> around my daughter.

Susan stands up.

> SUSAN
> Stephanie threatened to hurt
> you, you know. That's when I
> cut her off completely.

Marietta's eyes widen in surprise.

Susan calls over her shoulder as she goes upstairs.

> SUSAN
> Remember to feed and walk
> Jesse before you go to
> school.

Marietta restarts the video of Stephanie.

>   MALE STUDENT (voice)
> I think she's saying, like
> "baby" over and over. Fucking
> lunatic.

Snickers. The camera finds Marietta standing in the background, then goes back to Susan.

>   MALE STUDENT (voice)
> Look! She brought garbage bags
> full of sack lunch for me. I'm
> gonna take her home. My
> parents won't let me have a
> dog, but they'll let me have a
> bag lady.

>   MARIETTA (shouting)
> Leave her alone!

The video shows Marietta stomping away.

>   MALE STUDENT (voice)
> Hey, Marietta...

The school bell rings and the video ends.

Distracted, Marietta dumps half a bag of dog food into a shiny mixing bowl. She fills the plastic tub in the sink with water and shoves it all out of the patio door with her foot.

INT. RESTAURANT - NIGHT

Marietta and Roy sit at a table.

                    MARIETTA
          Dad, did Aunt Stephanie hate
          me?

Roy's hands still from cutting his steak.

                    ROY
          Stephanie had a hard of it
          time in life. She acted out
          her pain and anger because she
          didn't know a better way to
          deal. (starts cutting) She
          didn't hate you, though.
          (shakes head) No.

                    MARIETTA
          Is she happy now?

                    ROY
          I don't know, Marietta. I
          really don't. I'd like to
          think so.

                    MARIETTA
          Did anyone love her?

Roy puts down his knife and fork.

                    ROY
          Of course, honey. She was
          loved.

He picks up his glass of lemonade.

                    MARIETTA
          Did you love her?

Roy pauses for a long time, glass in the air. He finally remembers to take a drink and sets down the glass.

                    ROY (clearing throat)
          She was part of the family.

INT. SUSAN'S HOME:HALLWAY - NIGHT

                    ROY
          You'll be okay?

                    MARIETTA
          Dad, I'm sixteen, not six.
          Mom'll be back by ten.

                    ROY (laughing)
          Okay, I'm sorry. See you soon,
          sweetheart.

Marietta waves him away and closes the front door.

INT. SUSAN'S HOME:SUSAN'S BATHROOM - NIGHT

Marietta opens Susan's medicine cabinet and finds rows of mystery pharmaceuticals.

INT. SUSAN'S HOME:SUSAN'S BEDROOM - NIGHT

Taped to the back of a mirror, a restraining order.

Inside the night stand, a gun.

Marietta hears a car engine. Headlights beam into the room.

INT. SUSAN'S HOUSE:SUSAN'S CAR - NIGHT

From the driveway, Susan watches her bedroom light switch
off, expressionless.

INT. SUSAN'S HOUSE:MARIETTA'S ROOM - NIGHT

Marietta opens Stephanie's hidden journal again.

               STEPHANIE (voiceover)
          Papa was a superhero. I tell
          myself that. I like to think
          so. But he wasn't really. He
          was the Invisible Man eclipsed
          by Mama's so-called godly,
          goodly goodness.

On her tablet, Marietta plays more of the July 4th
barbecue.

Stephanie appears disheveled and wild-eyed.

               STEPHANIE (voice)
          Where's my baby? Where's my
          baby?

A couple of male relatives escort Stephanie out of the
backyard amid whispers of "drunk" and "high" and "crazy."

In her dreams, Marietta sees herself, then Susan, then
Stephanie.

               STEPHANIE (voiceover)
          Marietta! My baby!

Marietta wakes to hear Susan yelling up the stairs.

                    SUSAN
          Marietta! Wake up! You're
          going to be late for school!

Marietta looks at the clock and groans.

                    SUSAN (yelling)
          Marietta!

                    MARIETTA (yelling)
          I'm awake!

                    SUSAN (yelling)
          Marietta Brazil! You are
          supposed to feed and walk
          Jesse *every morning!*

INT. SUSAN'S HOUSE:MARIETTA'S BATHROOM - DAY

Marietta showers, scrubs a toothbrush through her mouth,
snaps a rubber band on her hair, then emerges from the
bathroom.

                    SUSAN (yelling)
          He's jumping around all over
          the kitchen. You need to…

                    MARIETTA (yelling)
          Mom, I'm coming!

Marietta rushes downstairs slinging her backpack over her
shoulder.

INT. SUSAN'S HOUSE:KITCHEN - DAY

Susan's bathrobe bears Jesse's paw prints. He's licking her face and hands. Disheveled, Susan knocks Jesse away. Jesse growls at Susan.

Marietta looks at the clock.

          MARIETTA
     Mom, I have to go. I'm late
     for class.

Marietta grabs fruit off the dining room table and heads for the front door while Susan tries to shove Jesse out the patio door.

          SUSAN
     No! Jesse, outside!
     Marietta…

Jesse barks in protest.

          SUSAN
     Marietta!

INT. SUSAN'S HOUSE:HALLWAY - DAY

Marietta stops with her hand on the front door.

INT. SUSAN'S HOUSE:KITCHEN - DAY

          SUSAN (yelling)
     Young lady, I told you about
     this!

Jesse growls louder at Susan's angry tone.

                    SUSAN (pointing)
          Jesse, go!

INT. SUSAN'S HOUSE:HALLWAY - DAY

                    MARIETTA
          Mom, just for today. Please?
          They make me stay after school
          every minute I'm late!

                    SUSAN (to Jesse)
          Get out!

Marietta shrugs and heads out the front door.

                    SUSAN
          Marietta!

EXT. SUSAN'S HOUSE:DRIVEWAY - DAY

Marietta pulls out of the driveway in an ancient station
wagon.

EXT. SCHOOL PARKING LOT - DAY

Marietta finds a photo of two babies in Stephanie's Bible.
On the back of the photo, "Alicia eighteen months" and
"Marietta fifteen months."

She finds another photo of Stephanie and Baby Alicia.

INT. SCHOOL LIBRARY - DAY

Marietta spins through the microfilm newspaper archive and finds, "Medical Coroner concludes accidental death of Baby Alicia."

"...Relatives of Stephanie and Alicia Madison voiced their agreement with the medical coroner's conclusion of the tragic, accidental death of Alicia Madison as a result of an unfortunate fall..."

INT. SUSAN'S HOUSE:KITCHEN - DAY

Susan scrubs Jesse's paw prints from the floor and sprays disinfectant everywhere.

INT. SUSAN'S HOUSE:BEDROOM - DAY

Intercut with

INT. ROY'S CONDO:HOME OFFICE - DAY

Clean and dressed, Susan puts on makeup and stretches her hair back into the tight bun.

She answers the phone when it rings.

>   SUSAN
> Oh. It's you.

>   ROY (sarcastic)
> Memories of our wedding vows.

>   ROY
> Susan, I'm worried about
> Marietta.

                    SUSAN
          Well, it's about time you
          worried about her. She's not
          taking care of that dog like
          she promised.

                    ROY
          No. I mean she asked me about
          Stephanie yesterday.

Susan sucks in her breath.

                    SUSAN
          What about?

                    ROY
          That got you, didn't it?

                    SUSAN
          Roy, don't start with me.

                    ROY
          Whether Stephanie was happy
          and did anyone love her.

                    SUSAN
          Well, I guess you would know
          the answer to that.

INT. SCHOOL LIBRARY - DAY

Marietta spins through more microfilm.

INT. SUSAN'S HOUSE:BEDROOM - DAY

Intercut with

INT. ROY'S CONDO:HOME OFFICE - DAY

> ROY
> Move on, Susan. This is no
> longer about you.

> SUSAN (contemptuous)
> No. It's about *you*. It's
> always been about you, Roy.

> ROY
> I think the Bible caused
> Marietta to think about it a
> little more.

> SUSAN
> What Bible?

> ROY
> She didn't tell you?

> SUSAN
> Tell me *what?*

> ROY
> Stephanie sent Marietta a
> Bible at my condo.

Susan walks downstairs with the phone.

                    SUSAN
          And you gave it to her, didn't
          you? *That's* the Bible Marietta
          carried to the funeral. I saw
          her   with   one   and   didn't
          think... Roy, we discussed
          this before. We weren't going
          to allow her...

                    ROY
          Susan, calm down! It was in
          the   wrapper. And it   was
          postmarked. I…

Susan's voice slices like a knife through the hallway.

                    SUSAN
          So why didn't *you* tell me?

                    ROY
          I didn't think it was that
          damn big a deal.

                    SUSAN
          You never do, Roy. Wait a
          second!

Susan drops the phone and shouts through the patio door.

INT. SCHOOL LIBRARY - DAY

Marietta stacks printouts and turns off the microfilm
reader.

INT. SUSAN'S HOUSE:BEDROOM - DAY

Intercut with

INT. ROY'S CONDO:HOME OFFICE - DAY

> SUSAN
> Let me call you back. Like I
> said, she has not been taking
> care of that dog. He's been
> barking all morning!

INT. SCHOOL CLASSROOM - DAY

Marietta hides her tablet behind her textbook and earbuds
behind her hair. She restarts the of July 4th video.

Susan weeps beautifully on Roy's shoulder.

Marietta shudders and pauses the video when the bell
rings.

INT. SUSAN'S HOUSE:KITCHEN - DAY

Jesse is quiet.

Susan dials Roy up and they continue the back-and-forth.

INT. SCHOOL CAFETERIA - DAY

Marietta sits alone at a lunch table with the Bible open.

           STEPHANIE (voiceover)
Mother slapped me at church.
She called me a blasphemer and
a liar.

Voices of other students drift over to Marietta's table.

           MALE STUDENT (voice)
That girl is fucking strange.
Why is she reading a Bible at
lunch?

           FEMALE STUDENT (voice)
Shhh! Her crazy aunt just
died.

           MALE STUDENT (voice)
Stephanie Madison's Last
Stand? That's the homeless
lady that used to stalk around
here!

           FEMALE STUDENT (voice)
Say it louder so she can hear
you, big mouth.

           MALE STUDENT (voice)
That's her aunt? No wonder she
spazzed. Fucking weird shit,
man.

Marietta quietly packs up her belongings and leaves the
cafeteria.

INT. MARIETTA'S CAR:ROAD - DAY

Marietta's on her cell phone and driving.

                    MARIETTA (shrieking)
What!

            ROY
Marietta, I'm your father. I
know you've been through a
lot. First Grandma, then Aunt
Stephanie… Now you're going
through puberty.

            MARIETTA
Dad. Are you kidding? Puberty
was four years ago.

            ROY
Well, it's that time in life
when everything changes.

            MARIETTA
Oh my God. Dad, please don't
put either of us through
this. I'm begging you.

            ROY
I'm just saying that you can
talk to me. I'm not trying to
be mean or anything. I'm just
concerned about your health.

            MARIETTA
Who told you I was on drugs?
I mean, where is this coming
from?

Marietta misses her turn and pulls over to the side of the
road.

INT. ROY'S CONDO:HOME OFFICE - DAY

       ROY
Your mother and I talked...

       MARIETTA
Mom? Mom told you I was on
drugs.

       ROY
Marietta…

INT. MARIETTA'S CAR:ROAD - DAY

       MARIETTA
Dad, drugs are stupid! I would
never do that, I promise!

INT. ROY'S CONDO:HOME OFFICE - DAY

       ROY
I know the separation must be
hard for anyone to understand.

       MARIETTA
But Dad, that's not...

       ROY
I promise you, Marietta, I'm
not going anywhere. We'll get
it all figured out real soon
and it's going to be okay.

INT. MARIETTA'S CAR:ROAD - DAY

After her father hangs up, Marietta sits a while.

> MARIETTA (whispering)
> What would you do, Stephanie?

She looks at Aunt Stephanie's Bible then opens it to a random page.

> STEPHANIE (voiceover)
> Arby used to look at me as if wondering the same thing. I hate that doubt in him. I hate my sister and the things she says and does. We can't choose our family. We just love our family. Or, at least, we tell everyone we do.

> MARIETTA
> Who's Arby?

Marietta scans the newspaper stories she printed.

> MARIETTA
> No Arby here.

She pulls out the tablet and restarts the July 4th video.

> MARIETTA (voice)
> Grandma, that was so weird.

> GRANDMA (voice)
> Susan works in mysterious ways.

Marietta shoves everything underneath her car seat and drives home.

INT. SUSAN'S HOUSE:MARIETTA'S BEDROOM - DAY

>   SUSAN (sorrowfully)
>   Your father is really not
>   himself lately. I think…
>   Stephanie's death affected
>   him more than he lets on.

Susan assesses Marietta.

>   SUSAN (sadly)
>   I've always had my suspicions,
>   you know. I heard the rumors.
>   The two of them. (pause)
>   Stephanie was... obsessed with
>   us. Me. Roy. You.

>   MARIETTA
>   Me? Why me? I never even
>   talked to her. You told me not
>   to.

>   SUSAN (nodding)
>   You represent the daughter
>   Stephanie always wanted but
>   wasn't woman-enough to raise.
>   You do know what really
>   happened to Baby Alicia, don't
>   you?

Marietta looks at her hands, nodding.

                    SUSAN
Stephanie has always been…
unwell, even when we were
children. No one in the family
trusted her. Even Roy. But I
think maybe, he still had
feelings. I know that she did.

                    MARIETTA (frowning)
What feelings?

                    SUSAN (smoothly)
But we always protected her.

                    MARIETTA
Mom, I don't think Aunt
Stephanie would have hurt me.

Jesse barks from the backyard. Susan looks out the window.

                    SUSAN (irritated)
Marietta, I grew up with
Stephanie. You're just a
child. You don't know her
like I did.

Susan waves away Marietta's protests.

                    SUSAN
        Yes, you are. You just don't
        understand. Stephanie couldn't
        function in normal society.
        She was hostile and paranoid.
        Couldn't hold a job. Couldn't
        hold a man. Or a baby. Dear
        God, she couldn't even handle
        a simple thing like reality.
        She thought she was some sort
        of freedom fighter.

Susan laughs and looks at Marietta.

                    SUSAN
        She was a drug mule! And then
        she just…

Susan turns away from the window and walks to Marietta's
mirror, speaking to her own reflection.

                    SUSAN
        That's why she died.

                    GRANDMA (voiceover)
        Susan works in mysterious
        ways.

                    MARIETTA (uneasily)
        Look, I mean… just as long as
        you know I'm not getting high,
        Mom.

Susan smiles, smooths her hair, turns away from the
mirror, sits back on Marietta's bed.

                    SUSAN
Of course not, Marietta. No
one who knows you and loves
you would ever believe
something like that.

Susan pauses as if a thought just occurs to her.

                    SUSAN
Oh yes. Your father did
mention one other thing--some
sort of gift you received
from Stephanie.

                    MARIETTA
Is that why you were in my
room?

                    SUSAN
Well, he was concerned that
you felt the need to be so
secretive about it.

                    MARIETTA
I wasn't being secretive. I
just didn't think it was
important.

                    SUSAN (pouncing)
Oh. Then can I see it?

                    MARIETTA
It's in my locker at school.
I'm... I'm still looking through
it.

                    SUSAN (assessing)
          At *school*. That's funny. I
          don't remember you showing
          such enthusiasm for the Good
          Book before. You told me that
          the kids at church were phony
          and fake.

                    MARIETTA
          Well, they are.

Marietta fiddles with objects on her nightstand.

                    SUSAN
          You'll never make any friends
          with that uppity attitude,
          missy. (laughs) Remember your
          sweet sixteen and that
          boyfriend you *nearly* had?

                    MARIETTA (hurt)
          Why are you bringing all that
          up? It was a long time ago and
          I don't care anymore. Nobody
          does.

                    SUSAN
          Own up to your mistakes,
          Marietta.

                    MARIETTA
          I'm more than the mistakes I
          made.

                    SUSAN
          No. You *are* the mistakes you
          made. We all are.

Marietta shakes her head.

>   SUSAN
>   Your father keeps trying to
>   please you despite it all. I'm
>   doing all that I can. Instead
>   of keeping your promises,
>   you're keeping secrets from
>   us.

Marietta shakes her head again.

>   SUSAN
>   When I think of all you could
>   be and choose not to, I lie
>   down and cry. Remember that
>   summer program?

>   MARIETTA (whispers)
>   Mom, you're not even allowing
>   me a chance, are you?

>   SUSAN
>   Determined to create a nervous
>   break-down out of thin air?

>   MARIETTA
>   I'm not! I'm just…

>   SUSAN
>   Calm down the hysterics,
>   Marietta.

>   MARIETTA
>   I'm not hysterical!

                    SUSAN (raising eyebrows)
          Aren't you? Can't you hear
          yourself? I think I'll have
          to talk to a doctor about
          your... behavior issues. I
          should have a long time ago.
          But we'll soon see.

                    MARIETTA
          Mom, being shy is not anti-
          social.

                    SUSAN
          And denial is not just a river
          in Egypt.

                    MARIETTA (shouting)
          I'm not in denial! I just…

                    SUSAN
          Sooo defensive, Marietta. (sly
          smile) As I've told you
          before, more listening, less
          talking.

Marietta stands up and backs away.

                    MARIETTA
          Stop it, Mom! Just stop!

                    SUSAN
          Marietta, I think you'd
          better calm down before you
          end up like Stephanie.

                    MARIETTA (screaming)
          No! No!

Marietta runs down the stairs.

>   MARIETTA (screaming)
>   Shut up! Shut up!

Susan shrugs and laughs when she hears the front door
slam. Then she looks towards the window when she hears
Jesse's barking.

EXT. SUSAN'S HOUSE:DRIVEWAY - LATE AFTERNOON

The sky is too dark. Thunder and lightning begins.

Jesse's still barking when Marietta screeches away in her
car.

INT. MARIETTA'S CAR - DUSK

Marietta sits in her school's empty parking lot surrounded
by a curtain of rain, lightning, and thunder.

She turns on the car's interior light and opens
Stephanie's journal.

>   STEPHANIE (voice)
>   Mama used to look at me so
>   sad like she wondered how
>   such a crazy child got in her
>   house and what should she do.
>   Nothing I said ever mattered.
>   She took the easy road and
>   thought the worst. Pretended
>   she didn't see. I AM NOT
>   CRAZY!!!

Marietta slams the book shut.

                    MARIETTA
          Stephanie...   Stephanie...
          that's why you sent the Bible
          to me! (pauses) I'm moving
          out. I'm gonna go home, pack
          up, and move out. Take Jesse
          with me. Live with Dad.

Marietta snaps on her seat belt.

                    MARIETTA
          She's a liar! All that stuff
          about Stephanie and Dad. Just
          four more months. I'll have my
          diploma. Leave home and never
          come back!

Marietta turns off the interior light and starts the car.

                    MARIETTA
          Suck it up and finish high
          school.

Marietta starts the windshield wipers.

INT. SUSAN'S HOUSE:KITCHEN - NIGHT

Lightning and thunder interrupt the pitch black night.

Susan sets something on a shelf. She wraps something into
a bundle.

INT. MARIETTA'S CAR - NIGHT

                    MARIETTA (sobbing)
          I'm not Aunt Stephanie!

Marietta wipes away tears and windshield fog.

EXT. SUSAN'S HOUSE:DRIVEWAY - NIGHT

In a dark raincoat, Susan walks towards the curb with the bundle.

INT. MARIETTA'S CAR:ROAD - NIGHT

                    MARIETTA
          She got Stephanie. She got
          Dad.   But   that   two-faced
          phony's not gonna get me.

EXT. SUSAN'S HOUSE:DRIVEWAY - NIGHT

Susan drops the bundle into the trash can at the curb and looks up when she hears a car engine.

INT. MARIETTA'S CAR:SUSAN'S HOUSE:CURB - NIGHT

The rain beats harder on the roof of the car.

                    MARIETTA
          Just stay calm is all.

Marietta squints and wipes windshield fog again.

EXT. SUSAN'S HOME:DRIVEWAY - NIGHT

Susan shoves the bundle further down into the trash can.

INT. MARIETTA'S CAR - NIGHT

                    MARIETTA (whispering)
          Maintain   your   composure,
          Marietta.

Headlights and lightning reveal Susan as a target (with
red smears on her cheek) through the rain.

Marietta gasps and slams the brake, except it is the
accelerator.

EXT. SUSAN'S HOME:DRIVEWAY - NIGHT

Susan screams.

Marietta screams and swerves.

INT. MARIETTA'S CAR:DRIVEWAY - NIGHT

Marietta lays across the car horn.

EXT. SUSAN'S HOUSE:DRIVEWAY - NIGHT

Susan lays across the driveway. Rain beats down upon Susan
without mercy.

INT. HOSPITAL:MARIETTA'S ROOM - DAY

                    MARIETTA
          Where am I?

                    ROY
          Marietta, honey, you're in the
          hospital.

Marietta's vision focuses on Roy, tired and grief-
stricken.

                    ROY
          Do you remember the accident?

                    Marietta
          Mom?

                    ROY (swallowing)
          Honey, Susan… Your mother is
          dead.

Marietta closes her eyes.

                    ROY
          You were hurt too.

Marietta lifts her head to see bandages wrapped around her
abdomen.

                    ROY
          Marietta, what happened?

                    MARIETTA (crying)
          Daddy.

Roy pushes a buzzer next to the bed.

                    MARIETTA
          Daddy. Daddy!

The nurse comes into the room at a run.

INT. HOSPITAL:HALLWAY - DAY

                    POLICE OFFICER (voice)
          We need a statement, sir.

                    ROY
          The statement is that a young
          and inexperienced driver had
          an accident under severe
          weather conditions. *That's*
          your statement.

                    POLICE OFFICER (voice)
          Sir...

                    ROY
          Now please allow my daughter
          time to recover from the death
          of her mother and her own
          injuries. She just had surgery
          yesterday.

                    POLICE OFFICER (voice)
          I'm just doing my job, sir. I
          mean, what with the
          restraining order against her
          sister and then the sister's
          death... (coughs) A neighbor
          observed Mrs. Brazil throwing
          food at the dog earlier that
          afternoon.

                    ROY
          Look, I'm not...

                    POLICE OFFICER (voice)
          The same neighbor reported
          screams and the dog barking
          about three hours later. Sir,
          does it concern you at all
          that the dog is still missing?

Roy stands up and spreads his hands.

                    ROY
          I can't do this right now.
          This is not going to happen
          today. Leave me alone. And
          leave my daughter alone until
          she heals.

                    POLICE OFFICER (voice)
          Sir, I apologize...

                    ROY
          Please, just go.

The Police Officer hesitates.

Roy moves to stand in the doorway to Marietta's room.

                    ROY
          Please.

                    POLICE OFFICER (voice)
          I'll be in touch. Thank you,
          sir.

INT. HOSPITAL:MARIETTA'S ROOM - DAY

Marietta overhears Roy's conversation with the Police
Officer, but pretends to be asleep when Roy looks in on
her.

INT. HOSPITAL:MARIETTA'S ROOM - DUSK

While Marietta sleeps, Roy takes the house keys from her
purse.

EXT. SUSAN'S HOUSE:ROY'S CAR - DRIVEWAY

Roy looks at the exterior of a dark, haunted house with
half-hearted crime scene tape and storm litter strewn
around the driveway.

Roy finds Susan's dirt and blood-covered clothing in the
trash can.

INT. SUSAN'S HOUSE:HALLWAY - NIGHT

Roy lets himself inside the house.

INT. SUSAN'S HOUSE:KITCHEN - NIGHT

Roy finds a flashlight in a drawer and a .38 special on
the shelf.

EXT. SUSAN'S HOUSE:BACK YARD - NIGHT

Roy searches the back yard and finds a freshly-dug mound
protected by the hedges.

INT. HOSPITAL:MARIETTA'S ROOM - NIGHT

Marietta speaks into the intercom.

                    MARIETTA (in pain)
          Nurse. Please help me. I need
          to find my Bible but I can't
          move.

The nurse enters the room with a ready smile.

                    NURSE (voice)
          I'm not surprised. After a
          transplant, the body needs
          plenty of rest in order to
          recover.

The nurse opens a small cabinet by Marietta's bed with
triumph.

                    NURSE (voice)
          Found it! Your father must
          have left it here.

                    MARIETTA
          Did you say transplant?

                    NURSE (voice)
          The steering wheel caused a
          lot of damage. One kidney. And
          the pancreas. They had to
          remove your spleen. But the
          doctors say you'll be fine.

Marietta stares blank-faced at the nurse.

                    NURSE (voice)
          Your mother, dear.

The nurse pats Marietta's hand and smooths the blanket.

                    NURSE (voice)
          She was an organ donor. Your
          father   approved   the
          operations since she was a
          close match (hesitates) Funny
          how life works sometimes.

Marietta stares at the ceiling.

                    MARIETTA
          Now, that *is* funny.

                    NURSE (voice)
          I'll give you a little
          something for the pain. Okay?
          Sleep for now.

                    MARIETTA (sneering)
          I'm a drug addict after all.
          Susan Brazil always gets her
          way.

INT. ROY'S CONDO:HOME OFFICE - DAWN

Roy's in the middle of a cell phone conversation.

                    VETERINARIAN (voice)
          We've seen this so many times
          before, there's no mistake.
          Definitely   positive.   I'm
          sorry.

                    ROY
          And the bullet wound?

                    VETERINARIAN (voice)
          One shot through the head.

Roy looks at Susan's gun on his desk.

                    ROY
          Stephanie's gun.

                    VETERINARIAN (voice)
          What was that?

                    ROY
          Nevermind. Look, Doc, I'd
          appreciate it if… you know.

                    VETERINARIAN (voice)
          I'm afraid not, Mr. Brazil. I
          don't know what happened, but
          I've already reported the
          gunshot to the police. Why
          didn't you bring this dog in
          for his vaccinations?

Roy disconnects the call and walks to his computer.

He types in a word, reads a paragraph, and cries.

INT. ROY'S CAR:ROAD - DAY

Roy tries to raise Marietta's doctor on his cell phone.

INT. HOSPITAL:MARIETTA'S ROOM - DAY

Marietta holds a sheet of paper.

STEPHANIE (voiceover)
I used to pretend that I'm
normal. I catch Susan's baby
before she falls. I have a
daughter and a man who loves
me. Every day, I try to be
better. But every day, someone
always reminds me and everyone
else of what happened. It was
an accident! I promise you!
Marietta was my niece and I
loved her too! I begged Susan
to forgive me, but she never
heard of that word. You were
the best thing that I ever did
with my life. I miss you so
much. But they said I had to
make it right. It is over for
me now. No more babies. I just
can't face it another day.
Even though Arby doesn't know,
I know you will be all right.
I love you, Alicia.

MARIETTA
No.

A creased, yellowed letter with shaky writing lays behind
that page.

GRANDMA (voiceover)
Trust in God, Stephanie.
Except His will be done. She
have took to Susan. She never
told you and Susan apart. You
will be blest and so will
she. We love you. Mama.

Marietta screams.

>   MARIETTA (crying)
>   Stephanie. Stephanie, it was
>   always you. All this time. It
>   was you!

Marietta cries and laughs from panic.

Voices overlap.

Marietta's nurse grabs at Marietta's wrist and leg.

Marietta sees Stephanie and Susan.

The doctor arrives to Marietta's room and shouts
instructions.

Roy bursts into Marietta's room after the doctor.

>   ROY
>   Marietta!

>   MARIETTA
>   Daddy... did you know? Did
>   you know what she did to me?

Marietta POV...

>   STEPHANIE
>   Is she happy?

>   SUSAN
>   I don't know. I really don't.
>   I'd like to think so.

Audience POV...

                    ROY
          Your mother? I know what
          happened to Jesse. I'm sorry,
          Marietta.

                    MARIETTA
          She's not my mother! I don't
          know who she is! I don't even
          know who I am. She did it to
          all of us.

                    ROY
          I found Jesse. She shouldn't
          have done that. Marietta, I'm
          sorry...

                    MARIETTA
          She did everything, Arby.

Marietta laughs hysterically.

The nurse yells at Roy, Marietta, and the doctor.

Marietta POV...

                    STEPHANIE
          Did anyone love her?

                    SUSAN (indignant)
          Of course! (accusingly) Did
          you love her?

Audience POV...

                    MARIETTA
No wonder we looked so much
alike. No wonder she was a
match. My mother's twin *would*
be a match. They exchanged me
like a sweater!

                    DOCTOR (voice)
Marietta, please calm down.

                    ROY (frantically)
Marietta, what are you...

                    MARIETTA (screaming)
I'm not Marietta!

                    DOCTOR (shouting voice)
Nurse! Get him out of here!

                    MARIETTA (screaming)
Did you know what they did,
Arby? Roland Brazil, did you
know? All of you lied to me.
All of you!

The nurse shoves Roy out of Marietta's hospital room.

Marietta POV...

Stephanie and Susan shush Roy and shoo him away.

                    MARIETTA (begging)
Who am I? Tell me. Whisper
it. I can keep the secret. I
can keep all the secrets. I
promise. Tell me who I am!

INT. ROY'S CONDO:HOME OFFICE - DAWN

Roy's computer screen shows a paragraph on Rabies.

INT. HOSPITAL:MARIETTA'S ROOM - DAY

Audience POV...

Marietta foams at the mouth. Her throat and jaw clench shut. The doctor and nurse try to shove a tongue depressor between Marietta's teeth.

Marietta POV...

Stephanie and Susan reach for Marietta while smiling.

           STEPHANIE, SUSAN
     You're part of the family.

Audience POV...

Marietta convulses and chokes on her tongue.

INT. HOSPITAL:HALLWAY - DUSK

           DOCTOR (voice)
     I'm sorry, Mr. Brazil. She
     never woke from the coma.

Tears roll down Roy's face. He buries his head in his hands.

INT. HOSPITAL:MARIETTA'S ROOM - DUSK

Roy pulls back the sheet that covers Marietta's face.

He sobs, then covers her again.

He notices the last page of Stephanie's journal and Grandma's letter beneath Marietta's hospital bed.

He reads everything.

EXT. HOSPITAL - NIGHT

A police office car pulls into the hospital parking lot and parks.

INT. HOSPITAL:MARIETTA'S ROOM - NIGHT

Roy pulls the thirty-eight special from his waistband.

He sits in the chair beside Marietta's bed to think things over.

INT. HOSPITAL:HALLWAY - NIGHT

          NURSE (voice)
     He's still in her room.

          POLICE OFFICER (voice)
     Thank you, Nurse. Just a few
     more questions to clarify some
     details.

There is a gunshot, surprised screams, and running feet

FADE OUT
THE END

Screenplay 2

The Lovebirds

CAST OF CHARACTERS

Abo/Able - West African, male, mid-30s to late 40s

Suma/Sammy - West African, male, 17

Nan - West African, female, mid-20s

Slavebreaker - Irish, male, late 40s

King (voice only) - West African, male, mid-60s

Slaver (voice only) - Portuguese, male, mid-40s

Auctioneer (voice only) - English, male, mid-60s

TIME
The story takes place on the western coast of 17th century
Africa and the eastern coast of 17th century America.

FADE IN

Title card shows the text:

> ABLE (voiceover)
> It was unspeakable, this thing
> done to kings and queens in
> the dark corners of the slave
> ships, in the holding cages of
> the slave factories, and in
> the dense forests surrounding
> the sugar and indigo
> plantations. For that reason,
> no one spoke of it.

INT. SLAVE CABIN - DAY

(SUMA) collapses into a sweaty, bloody, bruised heap in
the doorway of (ABLE'S) slave cabin.

He wears a rusted iron collar around his neck connected to
a heavy rusted iron chain.

A SLAVEBREAKER stands over Suma. A ring of skeleton keys
and a knife hang from his waistband.

The Slavebreaker spits on Suma's shaking form with
contempt.

> SLAVEBREAKER (voice)
> Take care of Sammyboy, Uncle
> Abe. He's a wild one, he is! A
> savage just off the boat.

Able stops tending to the fire and looks over his
shoulder.

                    SLAVEBREAKER (voice)
          But he'll soon learn his
          master. Or he'll die.

Suma screams something unintelligible.

The Slavebreaker kicks Suma in the abdomen.

Suma vomits.

                    SLAVEBREAKER (voice)
          What say he, Able? You speak
          that voodoo?

Able's shoulders sag. He bows his head.

Suma mutters again.

The Slavebreaker kicks Suma in the side again.

                    SLAVEBREAKER (voice)
          Sammyboy, you keep that tongue
          civil or we'll cut it out for
          you.

The Slavebreaker holds the knife up so Suma can see it.

                    SLAVEBREAKER (voice)
          What say he, Able? You
          understand him! Don't you
          pretend now.

Able frowns in diplomatic pretense of ignorance.

                    SLAVEBREAKER (voice)
          Able! Answer me! Be quick
          about it, damn ye. Or do ye
          need a turn in the barn as
          well? What say he?

                    ABLE
          Boss, he want the return of
          his charm, sir.

                    SLAVEBREAKER (voice)
          Charm, eh? That demon magic
          will not help him. This be a
          Christian land. D'ye 'ere
          that, monkey?

The Slavebreaker takes a small leather bag out of his
pocket and sprinkles the contents over Suma.

                    SLAVEBREAKER (voice)
          You mean this? You wish to
          charm us some more, eh? Then
          I'll be back for more!

The Slavebreaker snickers.

Suma clutches frantically at bird feathers and snake teeth
that float on the air and fall to the ground.

Able looks away.

                    SLAVEBREAKER (voice)
          Look at him play with his toys
          just like a little monkey!
          (laughs) Shut up now,
          Sammyboy. Or ye'll get more of
          what you already had and like
          it. Charm, indeed. Good fun,
          boy!

The Slavebreaker throws the empty bag at Suma and spits on
him again.

                    SLAVEBREAKER (voice)
           Fix 'im up, Uncle! Make 'im
           pretty for me now!

Able shudders in repulsion, but rises to obey.

EXT. COAST - DAY

Abo sweats and rows a smaller boat down a river with other
men.

The river empties to a lagoon and the lagoon drains to the
ocean

Portuguese voices shout threats and curses.

A gun barrel strikes Abo in the chest.

A large wooden boat sits on the ocean in the distance.

INT. SLAVE SHIP:HOLD - NIGHT

Abo lays squeezed on all sides inside a small, coffin-like
space.

His body is sweaty, dirty, covered in rat bites, and whip
welts.

Sounds of moaning, coughing, and vomiting surround him.

Rats chew on dead limbs.

EXT. SLAVE SHIP:DECK - DAY

Abo dances in leg irons on the ship deck.

When a whip lashes Abo, he dances faster.

Sounds of multiple splashes, then shouts.

Slavers look over the side and point.

Manacled hands embrace a slaver from behind and pull him overboard.

INT. SLAVE SHIP:DECK - NIGHT

White hands hold down writhing Black bodies--women and girls, men and boys--amid screams of horror and cries of pain.

Sounds of raucous Portuguese curses and laughter.

Abo stares in vacant shock surrounded by shadows of chaos.

Then, the bodies that surround Abo lay still as death.

EXT. SLAVE SHIP:DECK - DAY

Dead bodies hit the water.

Birds of prey screech and shark fins circle churning water.

>   ABLE (voiceover)
> By the time the ship reached
> this shore, I died a thousand
> deaths inside my own mind. My
> body, however, lived. There
> was really nothing more that
> they could do. But just to be
> on the safe side, they did so
> much more.

INT. SLAVE CABIN - DAY

>   ABLE
> Drink this.

Able holds the cup of water to Suma's mouth. He dips a rag into the water bucket to cleanse away dirt, sweat, blood, and whitish, viscous fluid from Suma's legs.

> SUMA
> No!

Suma snarls more in his own language and knocks Able's hands away.

> SUMA
> Unholy animal beasts of evil. Men who use other men like women in the land of devils. Defiled cannibals born of worms that eat excrement. I will kill them! Do you hear me, you old woman? I am a hunter for my people! I will kill them! And you too!

Able hands Suma the wet rag.

Suma knocks the rag out of Able's hand.

Able turns away.

EXT. AUCTION BLOCK - DAY

Able stands on the auction block. Excited voices jabber in English.

He looks up once with dead eyes and then focuses on the ground.

Screams echo inside Able's mind.

                    ABLE (voiceover)
          I pretended that I wasn't
          there. That this could not
          happen to me. The gods would
          not allow it. But once I
          learned to always expect the
          worst, I was never surprised
          or disappointed.

The English voice of the AUCTIONEER rings out.

                    AUCTIONEER (voice)
          Behold before you, King Able!
          This noble prince of the Dark
          Land is ready and willing to
          serve your every need. Strong,
          but humble! Large, but docile!
          He has been trained to follow
          every order and serve every
          need without question or dark
          look.

Dirty White hands gesture towards Able's wide shoulders.

                    AUCTIONEER (voice)
          Step closer for inspection! We
          run an honest business here,
          we do. Well suited for farms
          large or small. King Able
          lifts, carries, pulls, pushes,
          totes, and drags better than
          any horse!

Dirty white hands force Able's mouth open and run across
his teeth.

                    AUCTIONEER (voice)
          All teeth here!

Dirty, sweaty White hands run over Able's genitals and buttocks.

> AUCTIONEER (voice)
> Magnificent stud animal!

Able's eyes reveal fear and shame.

The White hands turn palm up with black smudges.

INT. SLAVE CABIN - DAY

> ABLE
> They hid the bruises with oil and dark powder. Their excitement was endless. They never tired. Like breaking a rebellious stallion or a wild bull. They wished to conquer me as a beast amid revelry and drink. Even when I submitted, they bruised me during... the domination to prove their power to me and each other.

> SUMA (disgusted)
> How can you bear to live? Why do you not die?

> ABLE (clears his throat)
> It is the peculiar way of this world, Sammy.

> SUMA
> You will call me by my name.

                    ABLE
What is your name?

        SUMA (draws up)
Suma. I am a hunter.

            ABLE
You will learn better, Suma.

        SUMA (suspicious)
How   is   it   you   know   my
language? You are not from my
people, but you know them.

            ABLE
I am an old man who barely
remembers a life before this
one. Who I used to be and what
I used to know was beaten to
the surface then bled to the
ground in the indigo fields
and the sugar plantations.

Able stares into the fire.

                ABLE
Some would say that is for the
best and what I deserve. You
ask me how I can bear to live.
My answer is I don't live. I
survive until I die.

            SUMA
Then why don't you kill
yourself?

                    ABLE
Maybe I am afraid of who waits
for me after death.

                    SUMA
You are not a man. You are a
coward. But aren't you still a
human being? Because if you're
no longer human, then what are
you?

                    ABLE
I am what they made me. I am
what you will soon become.

INT. KING'S COURTYARD - DAY

In a hall filled with carvings, statues, and weapons, Abo
and a statuesque African woman, NAN, stand side-by-side.

Abo draws himself up proudly.

                    ABO
Slavery is a tradition of war.
The conqueror always rules the
conquered. But now, the
conquerors do not come from
across the river or through
the jungle. They come in boats
from far away. They ask very
politely with guns drawn. If
we do not trade our rivals,
our rivals will trade us.

The KING makes no response.

                    NAN
We grow rich and powerful,
honored King. And we are
rewarded with weapons and
munitions and horses with
which to subdue and capture
our enemies. But instead of
carrying on the business of
farming, fishing, weaving, and
metalwork, the best of us
bring war to people with whom
we have no quarrel. We no
longer trade with the other
tribes. When there are no
others but ourselves left to
sell, then what shall we do?

Abo points an accusing finger at Nan.

                    ABO (outraged)
She dares to speak against
you, King, and to question
your decisions. How dare *she*,
a mere warrior…

                    NAN
I dare to speak for the future
before you destroy it for us
all.

                    ABO (scornful)
Her fear weakens us.

                    NAN
Your greed weakens us, Abo.

Nan turns back to the king anxious to appear the voice of reason.

> NAN
>
> We know of the Dark Queen of the South who fought the ghosts until the day she died. She refused to bow to their demands. It is possible to make a stand with the other tribes.

> ABO
>
> Great King, if we do not secure what the ghosts want from us, they will take us, instead. Even the Dark Queen knew this at the end. (pauses) Such treachery by Nan against the kingdom is punishable by death.

After a long pause, a deep voice answers.

> KING (voice)
>
> Do not forget your place, Abo. The honored King decides what is punished and how and why. Not you.

Abo bows his head.

                    KING (voice)
The foreigners wait at our
door like wolves with the
expectation that the king of
this land keeps his word. You
and Nan both agree that if our
people do not trade, then our
people will be traded.

Nan's mouth tightens, but she remains stoic.

                    KING (voice)
Nan, as the leader of the
warriors, your women will
protect Abo's raiders on this
mission against the northern
tribe. Upon your *victorious*
return, we will discuss
further various methods of
trade and industry.

A brief shadow crosses Nan's face.

                    KING (voice)
After that, you may convince
me of a better way, Nan.

Abo cannot help a smile of triumph.

                    KING (voice)
Abo, upon *your* victorious
return, you will have your
choice of the best land and
the best cattle... (pause) As
well as the best woman... to
reward your loyalty.

Abo turns his triumphant gaze back to Nan.

Nan stares back at Abo without expression.

INT. SLAVE CABIN - DAY

                SUMA
        Why do you waste my time with
        fairy tales? There has to be a
        way to escape this hell and
        return to our people, our
        land. Surely, you desire it.
        We can escape together!

                ABLE
        The way is too treacherous.

Suma repeats his curses and desperate incantations.

                ABLE
        Quiet, you fool! They'll hear!

Able checks the doorway, then returns to the fire.

                ABLE
        On the island where they took
        me, there were whispers of red
        people and black people that
        blended together. They fought
        the ghosts and remained free.
        Here, on this greater land,
        something similar happens.
        Once in a very great while, a
        slave or two or three vanishes
        in the night to the deep
        forests to the South. There,
        among the red people, they are
        kings and chiefs once more.

Suma stares into the fire.

>   SUMA
>   I want to go home, Able. I
>   want to see my own people
>   again. No more of this evil
>   world where men treat each
>   other like beasts.

Suma looks at Able with sadness.

>   SUMA
>   The   old   kingdoms   have
>   vanished,   you   know.   The
>   universities, the artwork, the
>   gold, the crafts… everything
>   is gone. What people of Home
>   used to be is legend now.

Suma returns his gaze to the fire as if hypnotized. His
voice slows and sing-songs from memory.

>   SUMA
>   The   lovebirds   rose   up   and
>   called to us to follow away
>   from danger. We sacrificed our
>   village to the God of Fire and
>   he protected us. The ground
>   shook under so many pounding
>   feet.

Abo's mouth drops open.

>   ABLE (whispering)
>   The lovebirds?

Suma remains fixated on the fire.

                    SUMA
The Snake gods would greet us
and we would either live or
die. But we would not be
captured. The song of the
lovebirds woke the Snake gods
in the deepest, darkest part
of the forest.

                    ABLE (choking)
Snakes!

                    SUMA
We followed fast behind
carrying Fire spirit which
warned the Snake spirits to
allow us passage. Through the
back of the Snake Kingdom a
small opening under the tree
roots was covered by rocks and
vines.

Able pays rapt attention.

SUMA

Upwards in darkness we crawled to the new tribe hidden on a high plateau of grass surrounded by trees and rocky cliffs, and covered by mists. We heard the screams of our pursuers and we celebrated. We were grateful and glad and gave proper thanks. The lovebirds, the snakes, and fire… our totems keep us safe and we will never return. I am the first child born to The Blessed of the Tribe of No Name.

ABLE (narrowing eyes)
Yet, you are here.

Suma looks at Able for a long moment.

SUMA
I am here, but not for long.

Suma looks at the fire again.

SUMA
Able, I can never return Home. That place is so far away and so dead now. (disgusted) But a man would rather die than remain here. So before I die tonight, tell me how to reach the Red Men of the South.

Able thinks that request over.

                    SUMA
Tell me now, Able! Right now!

                    ABLE
You   must   listen   to   me
carefully.

Suma nods.

                    ABLE
You   cannot   walk   away
unmarked. To escape from the
ghosts to the red tribes in
the darkest swamps, you will
have to fight the ghosts.
Maybe kill them. To kill
them, you will need their
weapons.

                    SUMA
How do I get them?

                    ABLE
You will need food to eat
along the way.

                    SUMA
I will steal it at night!

                    ABLE
At night. Yes, at night. That
will be the best opportunity.
When *he* comes for you again.

                    SUMA (scowling)
Who comes?

                    ABLE
That slavebreaker took a
liking to you, Suma. A real
liking. He will come again.
And again. And again. The
more you fight them, the more
they... want you. You fought
well. He will break your will
and then claim you as his own
special boy. But... in
time... he may treat you
well... if you treat him
well.

Suma cannot conceal an expression of utter repulsion from
Able.

                    SUMA (lip curled)   ,
What are you?

Able does conceals cold hatred for Suma behind a mask of
concern.

                    ABLE
What you will be. A survivor.

                    SUMA
I am not like you. I will
never be like you. I am still
a man. A hunter! I am the
First Born of the Blessed of
No Name. I am the hope of my
people.

                    ABLE
Not for very much longer.

                    SUMA
I will kill him where he
stands! Don't get in my way,
Able.

                    ABLE
Of course not... Suma. From
the   Slavebreaker,   take
weapons, clothing, everything.
Then run fast as you can. Run
far. South, always South.

                    SUMA
I will be free.

                    ABLE
Remember, you must give the
appearance of accepting your
position so he doesn't suspect
your true intentions.

                    SUMA (shudders)
I see.

                    ABLE
But there is more.

EXT. FOREST - DAY

Nan and Abo fight for passage through high grass and low-
hanging branches.

Nan carries bows and arrows, slingshots, and other weapons
on her back and waist.

                    ABO
You know this territory well,
Nan.

                    NAN
I serve the king well.

                    ABO
Perhaps   you   know   this
territory too well.

Nan is silent.

                    ABO
I am told by the wind of a
meeting between a warrior of
our kingdom and a sentinel of
the northern tribe.

Silence.

                    ABO
I am told that the meeting...
went… well.

Nan looks over her shoulder.

                    NAN
I don't like that ten of these
ghosts   come   with   us.   They
smell too strong. Talk too
loud. They slow us down. Why
don't they wait at the coast
for us to bring captives as
usual?

                    ABO
They insisted, Nan. As did our
king. Be careful.

                    NAN
          You are alive now because I am
          careful.

Abo bumps against Nan accidentally on purpose.

                    ABO (whispers)
          We both know you are the best
          woman of them all, Nan.

Abo bumps Nan again.

Nan stiffens. She raises her hand and makes a signal to
her warriors to spread out. The slavers and raiders do
likewise.

Nan moves to the far point position. Abo dogs her
footsteps.

Nan stumbles over a tree root jutting from the soil and
rolls two paces into a small tree filled with lovebirds.

The lovebirds rise and fill the air with distress calls.

                    ABO (hisses)
          Stupid bitch! They use the
          birds for warning!

Quick whistling *whisks* fill the air. Tiny darts come from
above in two directions.

Nan crouches at the base of the tree.
Two of Abo's raiders fall dead. Then two slavers fall.

One slaver screams outrage and shoots into the trees.

Silence.

Then *whisks*. The slaver with the gun falls dead.
Nan's warriors fail to find the target.

Abo doesn't join the fight. Instead, he kicks Nan, beats
her with his fists, then kicks her again.

> ABO
> You *never* fall, Nan. Never
> have I seen it. Treachery!
> What have you done to us? The
> king will know. He will know.

Another of Abo's warriors screams and writhes on the
ground.

A dart *whisks* by Abo's ear. Abo pulls Nan upright and
crouches behind her body with a knife to her back.

The attack ends. Nan signals her warriors forward.

> NAN
> After them!

Abo nods his head for his raiders to follow Nan's
warriors.

The slavers follow the raiders.

Abo throws Nan back to the ground and smiles down at her.

INT. SLAVE CABIN - NIGHT

> SUMA
> *You.*

                    ABLE
At first, they did not
recognize me, those empty
shells of the people I sold.
On the island, on the auction
block, and on the plantation
they shuffled with their eyes
on the ground. Because, that's
how slaves survive. We wear
masks of submission, fear, or
pleasure. Whatever it takes to
see another day. Once I put on
my own mask, I saw behind
theirs and they saw behind
mine and they celebrated and
gave thanks and were glad.
Just like your people, Suma--
The Northern tribe of No Name.

                    SUMA
The Jackal who Feasts on the
Dead. It's *you*... Abo.

                    ABLE
Abo died on the slave ship.
But Able stayed alive.

                    SUMA
Stayed alive to worship the
god of the ghosts, speak the
language of the ghosts, eat
the food of the ghosts, give
his body...

                    ABLE
A fool just like your mother.

Suma curses Able at the top of his lungs.

The slave cabin door bursts open.

The Slavebreaker's hand grasps the chain around Suma's neck and yanks him out of cabin.

> SLAVEBREAKER (voice)
> Ye still haven't learned, boy.
> We'll work hard to break ye,
> but break ye we will, by God!

EXT. PLANTATION - NIGHT

The Slavebreaker drags Suma towards the barn.

INT. BARN - NIGHT

The Slavebreaker triple wraps the chain on Suma's neck to a structure peculiar to slave torture.

INT. SLAVE CABIN - NIGHT

Abo drinks from a bottle of liquor.

INT. BARN - NIGHT

The barn door opens and closes several times amid the sounds of Suma's screams and male laughter.

INT. SLAVE CABIN - NIGHT

Able smiles in a stupor. Another rum bottle hits him in the chest.

> SLAVEBREAKER (voice)
> Be a good boy and clean him up
> again, Uncle Abe. Be quick
> about it now! He's nicely
> broken in, he is. Settled down
> a bit. We'll trade him in the
> morning.

INT. BARN - NIGHT

Covered in a muddy mixture of dirt, urine, blood, sperm,
and saliva, Suma lays amid the manacles in the straw.

He stares with a blank expression at the straw.

The barn door opens again.

Horses snuffle. A barn owl hoots.

EXT. FOREST - DAY

Abo rises from Nan's violated body to follow the slave
raiding party to the empty village, a blazing inferno.
Smoke fills the air.

He surveys the damage.

> ABO (muttering)
> They had warning.

Two of his raiders and three slavers run into the empty
village. They hold two of Nan's warriors with them.

They shout for Abo to run. Abo runs with the group back to
the clearing.

                    SLAVER (Portuguese voice)
          We followed their trail from
          the burning village to a dark
          canopy of trees that attacked
          us with black magic! Pure evil
          hissed at us and the trees
          threw vipers from every
          direction. The devil in the
          forest swallowed seven warrior
          women whole. We barely saved
          these two! What bloody hell
          was that you led us to Abo?
          Mother of God what deviltry is
          this that causes an evil tree
          to throw poison thorns, turns
          people into snakes and then
          eats people?

Abo looks at them as if they've gone bonkers. Then he
stares at the trampled grass, disturbed earth, and bird
feathers.

                    ABO (shouting)
          She's gone! Do you hear me?
          She's gone! Where did she go?

Abo backhands one of the two remaining warriors.

                    ABO (shouting)
          Where is she?

The slavers, seeing Abo's agitation catch on quickly.

                    SLAVER (Portuguese voice)
The evil witch leader led us
through her snake forest into
the very mouth of her Dark
Master. (spits) We're well rid
of her.

                    ABO (halting Portuguese)
We were gone long enough for a
leopard to carry her off.
(pause) I should have known
she was a traitor!

                    SLAVER (Portuguese voice)
Yes, Abo. You should have
known.

He turns his gun on Abo.

                    SLAVER (Portuguese voice)
You will take their place.

The other two slavers hold the remaining warriors and
raiders at gunpoint and collect their less lethal
weaponry.

INT. BARN - NIGHT

Suma closes his eyes.

                    NAN (voice)
Abo, the Jackal, who feasts on
rotten   flesh...   Abo,   the
Hyena, Who Would Sell His Own
Mother... Abo the Shadow, who
disappeared   into   the   wooden
bellies,   swallowed   by   the
ghosts of the ocean, never to
be seen again...

                    SUMA
Abo. (laughs) Abo! Abo! You
are real. Real!

INT. BUNKHOUSE - NIGHT

The Slavebreaker and his colleagues relive the night's
adventure with Suma with jokes and laughter and rum.

                    SLAVEBREAKER (voice)
          Here now. Hold on!

INT. BARN - NIGHT

Able walks closer to Suma and sips from a large bottle of
rum.

                    ABLE
I developed an appetite for
rum long ago when the
foreigners first came to flash
their guns and mirrors and
bottles of liquid fire. When
my gods turned their backs on
me, I did likewise. This
bottle (holds up bottle) is my
god now and brings me peace.

                    SUMA
They told me to never leave
the plateau to hunt. But there
was no more game on the
plateau.

                    ABLE
You look… just like your
mother.

Suma looks up at Able.

In no hurry, Able takes another drink.

                    ABLE
The sentinels came back for
her, didn't they?

                    SUMA
My father.

          ABLE (laughs)
Your father. Really.

                    SUMA
A great man, who would spit in
your face and gut you with a
knife for all the evil that
you have done.

                    ABLE
Yes. I do believe he would...
if he could.

INT. BUNKHOUSE - NIGHT

                    SLAVEBREAKER (voice)
One of ye daft buggers stole
me Grandad's knife. I'll have
it back, gents! Ante up!

A chorus of "no, no" and shouts of ridicule answer the
Slavebreaker.

INT. BARN - NIGHT

Able crouches by Suma and talks quietly in his ear.

ABLE
The King himself agreed that
those of his people who made
such serious miscalculations
deserved to take the place of
the thirty villagers of the
northern tribe he'd promised
to the ghosts. The ghosts
demanded compensation under
threat of the gun and a
promise to enforce future
transactions. And so, the
ghosts did not waste a trip.
But neither did they venture
into the interior again.

SUMA
Not for another seventeen
years.

ABLE
Your mother betrayed an entire
kingdom.

SUMA
She saved an entire people.

Able moves closer to intimidate and demoralize Suma.

ABLE
Yet, Suma, you are here.

EXT. BARN - NIGHT

The Slavebreaker staggers to the barn door.

                    SLAVEBREAKER
          Damn me eyes, I left me keys
          too!

The Slavebreaker pounds on the barn door.

INT. BARN - NIGHT

                    SUMA
          I am here. But, at last, I
          know the reason why.

Suma thrusts the knife he slipped from the Slavebreaker's
waistband into Able's abdomen like a snake bite.

Able gasps in shock and pain.

                    SUMA (whispering)
          I am still a man. Man enough
          to do the demon the one favor
          he cannot do for himself.

After a lot of pounding, the barn door opens.

Able laughs a little.

Though exhausted from breaking into the barn and drunk
from the rum, the Slavebreaker's eyes widen.

Suma stares Able full in the face.

                    SUMA
          I am the First Born of the
          Blessed.

The Slavebreaker takes a deep breath to sound the alarm on
Suma's attack on Able.

EXT. FOREST - DAY

Lovebirds fly up.

Wings beat the air.

Feathers fall.

Birds cry in alarm.

INT. BARN - NIGHT

Cold moonlight shines throughout the interior of the barn.

An orange glow warms the barn's interior and grows stronger, redder.

Wooden doors bang open. Excited horses and cattle shriek.

Two empty rum bottles break into shards as the fire swallows them.

Injured, drunken Able comes to and grunts as the fire licks his feet.

Able screams for help and looks around.

Beside Able, the Slavebreaker's legs and torso are stripped bare.

The heavy chain coils around his neck like a snake. Skeleton keys lay beside the chain.

The Slavebreaker's eyes and tongue bulge from his blue face.

Able's screams are lost amid the screams of horses and cattle, and pounding hooves.

EXT. PLANTATION - NIGHT

Horses and other animals race every direction from the burning barn.

EXT. FOREST - NIGHT

Boots pound through underbrush.

Legs dressed in the Slavebreaker's pants and arms dressed in the Slavebreaker's shirt pump the air for greater speed.

One hand holds a knife.

The boots stop running. The legs and arms still.

Suma looks back.

EXT. PLANTATION - NIGHT

A wild red inferno roars up to a black sky.

The barn's roof caves in.

The fire spreads.

White men and Black slaves run around.

Some slaves remain to help. Others dash off into the night.

EXT. FOREST - NIGHT

Suma lifts his arms to feel the Southern wind.

Then he runs faster into the night.

FADE OUT
THE END

Screenplay 3

Davey in The Lying Time

CAST OF CHARACTERS

Davey - Black American, Female, 30-35

El Leo - Mexican, Male, 45-50

Jace - Male, 30-40

Minister Martinez - Mexican American, Male 45-50

Dennis - Black or Mexican American, Male, 30-40

Congressman (voice only)

News Reader (voice only)

Time
Present day.

FADE IN

INT. TEXAS-MEXICO BORDER:MAQUILADORA - DAY

EL LEO, seated behind a desk with a sword, chuckles to himself.

MINISTER MARTÍNEZ and DAVEY stand in front of El Leo.

>   EL LEO
>   Were you born an American,
>   Minister Martínez?

>   MIN. MARTÍNEZ
>   Yes.

>   EL LEO
>   Where?

>   MIN. MARTÍNEZ
>   El Paso.

>   EL LEO
>   A Texan. How about you,
>   Miss...

>   DAVEY (defiant)
>   Dallas.

Davey stares at El Leo coldly.

>   EL LEO
>   Two Texans! The cowboy and his
>   cowgirl from the Wild West. JR
>   Ewing. The land of oil and
>   greed. Texas was a slave state
>   prior to America's own Civil
>   War. With great fields of
>   cotton picked by I believe it
>   was, slaves. Am I right,
>   Minister?

>   MIN. MARTÍNEZ (voice)
>   That's true, for a brief
>   period.

El Leo looks Davey and the Minister over and notices that
they both wear crosses.

El Leo returns focus to the Minister and straightens the
sword on his desk.

>   EL LEO
>   I can see that you are of
>   mixed race, Señor. Would it
>   not be a most intriguing
>   irony to learn that your
>   White ancestors once owned
>   Miss Dallas's Black
>   ancestors? And now you are
>   here to make amends by
>   teaching Miss Dallas how to
>   set slaves free... on the eve
>   of America's Independence
>   Day, no less.

Min. Martínez remains silent.

INT. DALLAS:DENNIS'S APARTMENT - NIGHT

JACE enters the doorway invading DENNIS'S space.

>   JACE
>   Mighty quiet all by yourself.
>   I guess you're running the
>   whole show with Martínez and
>   Davey lost in Mexico.

>   DENNIS
>   I already told you on the
>   phone that I don't know
>   what's going on. I have no
>   idea where they are or what
>   happened.

                    JACE
Not even one idea? Dennis
shakes his head as Jace moves
closer.

                    JACE
No clue, huh? Not the
slightest idea. Not even a
teeny, tiny, little speck of
an idea.

Dennis blinks.

Jace stalks and circles Dennis around the room.

Dennis flinches and backs away.

                    JACE
How about a guess? Just, throw
out your wildest theory. Your
boss and co-workers went to
free trafficked women at the
border. The co-workers are
dead. Davey and Martínez are
missing. Made any calls? Found
out anything official?
Contacted any embassies? No?
Nothing? Not a single thing?

INT. TEXAS-MEXICO BORDER:MAQUILADORA - DAY

                    EL LEO
You must feel at home in
Mexico, Minister Martínez. It
is not so different, I think.
Do you like it here? You are
here. Therefore, you must
surely like it here.

INT. DALLAS:DENNIS'S APARTMENT - NIGHT

Jace backs Dennis into a corner.

>   JACE
> That twinkle in your eye that
> tells me you're about to piss
> in your pants also tells me
> you know something. I wanna
> know something too, Dennis.

INT. TEXAS-MEXICO BORDER:MAQUILADORA - DAY

El Leo speaks to Minister Martínez.

>   EL LEO
> You've already experienced so
> much of the joy and pain there
> is to find in the desert. Your
> unfortunate pain. My ever-
> lasting joy. There is not much
> else to know... except that...

El Leo looks at Davey and slides the sword a little closer
to him.

>   EL LEO
> ...sometimes it is right to
> kill. To defend. To protect.
> To achieve. That should be
> understood above all else.

Davey looks at the sword.

INT. DALLAS:DENNIS'S APARTMENT - NIGHT

>   DENNIS
> It's not my fault!

Jace lays his police badge on the desk.

                    JACE
          What have you done?

Something catches Jace's eye.

INT. TEXAS-MEXICO BORDER:MAQUILADORA - DAY

El Leo focus back on Minister Martínez and rises.

                    EL LEO
          My highest regards to your
          Brother Dennis.

Davey stares, horrified at El Leo's cruel smirk.

El Leo holds the sword aloft.

Davey's eyes well up with tears.

                    MIN. MARTÍNEZ
          Davey, don't cry.

Davey looks pleadingly at El Leo.

                    DAVEY
          Please don't do this.

El Leo looks at Davey with concern.

                    EL LEO (disgusted)
          You see? *This* is what he says
          when life is at stake. When
          the blade of the sword is at
          his   throat.   When   he   looks
          into a man's eyes and sees El
          Diablo   staring   back   from
          inside that man's skull, he
          says   (mimicking)   "Davey,
          don't cry." (to the Minister)
          That's all you have to offer
          her?

Davey shakes her head.

> DAVEY (crying)
> No. Don't. Don't!

> El LEO (disappointed)
> You deserve so much better,
> Davey.

> DAVEY (begging)
> Please. Please, don't do
> this. Please.

> El LEO
> You will now learn from the
> best teacher of all, Davey.
> The Devil himself.

> DAVEY (wailing)
> No! No!

El Leo decapitates Min. Martinez.

Davey screams.

INT. DALLAS:DENNIS'S APARTMENT - NIGHT

Jace towers over Dennis, seated at his desk.

Jace shoves a photo of Minister Martínez, Davey, Dennis,
and other missionaries in Dennis's face.

Dennis has circled himself and Davey with a heart shape.

> JACE
> Davey didn't want a lying
> snake, did she? You couldn't
> have her, so you sold her.

> DENNIS
> They were to be held. That's
> it!

                    JACE
          Wow. Not so tiny an idea
          after all. Now we're getting
          somewhere. Then what? You'd
          raise the alarm and get a
          rescue going? Then what?
          You'd be her hero and she'd
          run into your arms? That the
          big plan?

Jace follows Dennis's glance downward to the desk. Jace
snatches up a scratch pad with numbers on it.

                    JACE
          Ah, the hero keeps his eyes
          on the prize.

Jace's eyes grow cold. He taps the scratch pad.

                    JACE
          What's this figure?

                    DENNIS
          He wasn't supposed to kill
          anyone.

                    JACE
          He *who*, you snake!

Dennis hesitates.

Jace slams Dennis's head against the desk.

Dennis sobs in pain and fear.

                    JACE
          Answer!

INT. TEXAS-MEXICO BORDER:MAQUILADORA - DAY

El Leo smiles at Davey's horrified sobs and the blood
spattered across her face.

                    EL LEO
Minister Martínez is home
now. He will always be part
of Mexico.

INT. DALLAS:DENNIS'S APARTMENT - NIGHT

                    DENNIS
When I asked them about the
killings, they said they
would kill me too if I told.

                    JACE
Ah! No. Is that what has you
all upset, Dennis? Look, it's
gonna be okay. It's gonna be
all right. They won't kill
you. No. I'm not gonna let
them. They won't get anywhere
near you. You see, cause
(pause) I wanna do that.

Jace sounds like a pleasant television ad from a
pharmaceutical company.

                    JACE
Are you having difficulty
breathing? Seeing spots in
front of your eyes? Is your
heart pounding? Are your
lungs bursting? That feeling…
that feeling, Dennis… is
death. Can you taste death
bubbling up in the back of
your throat? Kind of acid?
Kind of acrid and sour? Tell
me about death, Dennis. Tell
me. How does it feel? How
does death taste?

Dennis gasps and gags.

                    JACE
          TELL ME! Who?

                    DENNIS
          You can't do this to me.

                    JACE (laughing)
          But, yet, I seem to be doing
          it. You believe in God.
          Maybe... it's a miracle.

Jace tightens his grip and shakes Dennis like a rag doll.

                    JACE
          Answer!

                    DENNIS (coughing)
          El Leo. The Lion.

INT. TEXAS-MEXICO BORDER:MAQUILADORA - DAY

El Leo holds the sword aloft then swings chopping off part
of Davey's braids.

Davey screams.

                    EL LEO
          Your first lesson. Killing's
          easy, Miss *Davey* the Dallas
          Cowgirl. With practice, it
          gets easier.

He scrapes the sword up and down Davey's neck softly
leaving marks.

                    DAVEY
          Oh God, please help me.

Davey cries from pain, terrorized and broken down.

INT. DALLAS:DENNIS'S APARTMENT - NIGHT

           JACE
I'll bet even the Devil hates
you.

INT. TEXAS-MEXICO BORDER:MAQUILADORA - DAY

           EL LEO
No. *Not* God. You see, there
has been a misunderstanding
that I really must clear up
with you. You and your people
came down here with your God.
But this territory is already
occupied. *I* will be the one
to introduce you to our
(pause) special ways. Not
you. And not your God either.

El Leo snatches the crucifix from Davey's neck.

INT. DALLAS:DENNIS'S APARTMENT - NIGHT

           JACE
Don't you go anywhere,
Dennis. If you run, I'll find
you. And if I don't, though I
will, certain people with
considerable resources will
find you as well. And then,
there's El Leo. Stay right
here, Dennis.

INT. TEXAS-MEXICO BORDER:MAQUILADORA - DAY

El Leo lowers the sword and speaks over Davey's shoulder.

                    EL LEO
          Take him away. Bury him deep
          into Mexico so that he knows
          he is home again.

There is a dragging noise.

The minister's crucifix lays in a pool of blood.

Davey stares at the wall, almost catatonic.

                    EL LEO
          At last, we're alone. You
          know what happens now, don't
          you?

Davey doesn't respond.

El Leo smiles and shakes his head.

                    EL LEO
          So much to learn.

EXT. DALLAS:JACE'S CAR:ROAD - NIGHT

Jace calls the Congressman from his car.

                    JACE
          El Leo has her. I'm on my way
          to the border. Dennis sold
          them all out for a percentage
          of ransom.

                    CONGRESSMAN (voice)
          El Leo? Jesus. The Lion is a
          psychopath. He's a monster.
          Jace, I have to warn you, he
          sells women with the guns and
          drugs. Do you understand what
          that means?

                    JACE
          I'm going to get her back,
          Congressman. I need your help
          to operate in Mexico. You owe
          me.

                    CONGRESSMAN (voice)
          I can get you across the
          border and then get you
          weapons. That's it. I can't
          take the blow back just
          because you're sentimental.

EXT. DALLAS:JACE'S CAR:ROAD - NIGHT

                    JACE
          You have to pay the cost to
          be the boss, Congressman.

                    CONGRESSMAN (voice)
          Oh, how well I know. I'll do
          it on one condition. El Leo's
          a valuable asset. Get him too
          and bring him back alive.

                    JACE
          Fuck!

INT. TEXAS-MEXICO BORDER:MAQUILADORA - DAY

Naked, Davey kicks El Leo hard in the groin, then cuts off
his scream with a blow to the throat.

Davey throttles El Leo with her bra. Her shirt and pants
are torn and scattered about the room.

She takes El Leo's clothes and radio and hides behind the
door with the sword at the ready.

There is a male shout.

Davey swings the sword through the doorway. Blood sprays on her.

Davey collects her victim's equipment.

She repeats the procedure with the next man and collects more equipment and keys.

INT. TEXAS-MEXICO BORDER:MAQUILADORA - DAY

Her face covered with blood, Davey makes her way to a large truck.

She works her way through sets of keys, starts the truck, and pulls away in a cloud of dust.

INT/EXT. JACE'S CAR:MEXICO - DUSK

Jace recognizes Davey and blocks the road.

Davey cocks a gun, braced for another fight.

                    JACE
              Davey!

Davey and Jace race to hug each other.

                    JACE
              Where is he Davey? Is El Leo
              behind you?

A hardness settles into Davey's face.

                    DAVEY
              He's dead. I killed him.

Jace notices the blood on Davey's face, the shadows in her eyes, and the deadness in her voice.

He swallows.

Davey sees the judgment in his expression and it breaks her heart.

> JACE
> Martínez? The others?

Davey shakes her head. Her eyes well with tears.

> JACE
> Come on. We're getting out
> of here.

INT/EXT. JACE'S CAR:MEXICO - DUSK

> DAVEY
> What about border patrol? I
> don't have identification.
> (whispering) They took
> everything.

> JACE
> It's handled. Look, I don't
> know what happened out there,
> Davey. What they did to
> you...

Jace gestures at Davey's neck wound. Davey looks away and shakes her head.

> DAVEY
> El Leo killed Minister
> Martinez. Everyone. They're
> all dead. All of them.
> Slaughtered like animals.
> Covered with ants.

Tears roll down Davey's face.

> JACE
> What about you?

> DAVEY
> I'm alive.

                    JACE
          What did he do to you,
          Davey?

Davey doesn't answer.

                    JACE
          Why did he keep you alive and
          kill the men?

Davey closes her eyes.

                    JACE
          What happened?

                    DAVEY (screaming)
          I'm alive!

                    JACE
          I'm here now, Davey. I won't
          leave you. I'll always love
          you. No matter what.

Davey stares out of the car window.

                    DAVEY (quietly)
          Don't ask me again.

With the Congressman's machinations, Jace and Davey make
it past border control back to Texas.

INT/EXT. TEXAS:JACE'S CAR - DUSK

Jace calls the Congressman.

                    JACE
          I have her. We're back across
          the border.

                    CONGRESSMAN (voice)
          El Leo?

Jace eyes Davey.

                    JACE
          He's dead. I killed him.

Davey gives Jace a strange look.

                    CONGRESSMAN (voice)
          Which means you didn't meet
          the condition.

                    JACE
          The situation was difficult.
          It couldn't be helped.

                    CONGRESSMAN (voice)
          And now, neither can you. You
          cost my people an asset,
          Jace.

                    JACE
          I'll be back in Dallas in a
          few hours.

                    CONGRESSMAN (voice)
          Then you will see me soon.

INT. DALLAS:DAVEY'S APARTMENT - NIGHT

Davey emerges from the shower.

                    DAVEY
          Jace, I...

                    JACE
          I have to meet someone.

Davey blinks.

Jace kisses Davey good-bye.

                    DAVEY
          Jace, wait.

Jace smiles and hugs her.

> DAVEY (whispers)
> Don't act like we'll never
> see each other again.

Jace pulls away.

> JACE
> I have to go now, Davey.

Davey sits on the bed, stunned.

> DAVEY
> I did what I had to do, Jace.

> JACE
> Don't leave the apartment.
> It's not safe.

Jace stops at the door and speaks over his shoulder.

> JACE
> Davey, I would die for you
> just to make it all go away.
> Even to stop it from ever
> happening in the first place.

> DAVEY
> Don't leave me.

Jace leaves.

INT. DALLAS:DENNIS'S APARTMENT - NIGHT

Davey, with a bandage on her neck, enters Dennis's door.

> DENNIS
> Davey. I'm so glad you got
> out okay. I was worried and I
> told...

The television is on.

>   NEWS READER (voice)
>   ...says   that   it   is   not
>   patriotic   to   use   fireworks
>   irresponsibly.

>   DENNIS
>   Oh   my   God,   your   arm!   Can   I
>   get   you   anything?   Some
>   aspirin?

>   DAVEY
>   This won't take long.

INT. DALLAS:JACE'S CAR - NIGHT

Jace drives with purpose.

>   CONGRESSMAN (voiceover)
>   Her   record   as   a   juvenile
>   delinquent   and   former   gang
>   member   entered   the
>   discussion.

INT. DALLAS:DENNIS'S APARTMENT - NIGHT

>   DENNIS
>   I've   just   been   trying   to
>   straighten   out   some   paperwork
>   regarding   the   mission.   It's   a
>   complete mess.

>   DAVEY
>   Must be hard on you.

Davey sees a half-packed suitcase through the bedroom
door.

>   DENNIS
>   Don't get me wrong. I know
>   that pales in comparison.

                    DAVEY
          So pale it's invisible. There
          is no comparison, Dennis.

                    DENNIS
          Davey-

Davey steps closer to Dennis, seated at his desk.

                    DAVEY
          Why did you do it?

INT. DALLAS:JACE'S CAR - NIGHT

Fireworks.

                    CONGRESSMAN (voiceover)
          They found her identification
          and two crucifixes from the
          mission at the kill site.
          Hers and the minister's. The
          word 'terrorism' was
          mentioned more than once. You
          were her arresting officer,
          you know what she is.

Jace shakes his head.

INT. DALLAS:DENNIS'S APARTMENT - NIGHT

                    DAVEY
          Was there that much hate
          inside you, Dennis?

                    DENNIS
          Davey, you don't understand.

                    DAVEY
          No. *You* don't understand. You
          didn't see the look in his
          eyes...

                    DENNIS
          Davey, it wasn't like that.

Davey hits him across the face. Tears roll down her
cheeks.

                    DAVEY
          Shut up! I'll tell you what
          it was like. He knew. Right
          before El Leo (swallows),
          before he... Minister
          Martínez knew it was you. El
          Leo told us.

                    DENNIS
          Davey, I didn't know! It was
          all a mistake. It wasn't
          supposed to… what they said…

                    DAVEY (incredulous)
          A mistake?

Davey laughs in disbelief.

INT. DALLAS:JACE'S CAR - NIGHT

Fireworks.

                    CONGRESSMAN (voiceover)
          We need a body, Jace. I don't
          care whose it is. Yours,
          hers, whoever's. The cartels
          are not going to let this go.
          We need someone *tonight* to
          pay the bill. After it's
          done, you don't wear that
          badge ever again.

                    JACE (voiceover)
          I already know how the story
          ends, Congressman.

> CONGRESSMAN (voiceover)
> No. I don't believe you do.

Jace guns his car engine and speeds around street corners.

INT. DALLAS:DENNIS'S APARTMENT - NIGHT

Davey takes a step closer to Dennis who backs up and sits at his desk.

Davey flicks her eyes past Dennis's head and sees a passport and an airline ticket on the desk.

> DAVEY
> You knew they would die. You researched everything and set it up. You knew what kind of people we were dealing with and you didn't warn us. You knew what he would do to me.

> DENNIS (horrified)
> No!

> DAVEY
> Yes! "People will steal, kill, and cheat to protect their money. Don't be fooled by hidden agendas." That's what you said about El Leo, but that's really when you told us who *you* were.

Dennis is silent.

Tears come to Davey's eyes although her voice is cold.

                    DAVEY
They screamed, you know. They
cried for help. They (gasping
sob) begged to live. Then
they lay there dying while
they were robbed and kicked
and spat on. It wasn't brave
or noble. It was the ugliest,
dirtiest, filthiest thing
I've ever seen. The ants
swarmed all over them. Those
men had families.

                    DENNIS
Davey, please understand.

Fireworks.

                    NEWS REPORTER
The individual names of the
Christian missionary group
from Dallas recently killed
at the Mexico border are
withheld until the next of
kin are alerted…

                    DAVEY (sorrowfully)
You knew… as will others.

Davey sees Dennis's photograph of the mission group and
understands what the heart symbol means. She gasps with
repulsion.

Dennis looks wild-eyed.

Davey sees something horrible in his face and backs away.

Between firework explosions, there is a scream then a
gunshot.

INT. DALLAS:JACE'S CAR - NIGHT

> CONGRESSMAN (voiceover)
> The bodies will be flown back
> this week. But we need a body
> *tonight*. Give us a body for
> the cartel. That's how the
> story ends.

Jace sighs.

Jace parks in front of Dennis's building and checks his
weapon.

He lays his badge on the car seat.

Fireworks.

INT. DALLAS:DENNIS'S APARTMENT - NIGHT

Dennis sits at his desk, head in hands.

> NEWS REPORTER
> While the death of the
> leader, El Leo, is confirmed,
> the identity of the person
> who ended his life is not yet
> known, but Mexican officials
> are leading the
> investigation...

A gloved hand pushes the knob of Dennis's door.

> NEWS REPORTER
> ...the Congressman expressed
> his heartfelt sympathies for
> the families directly
> affected by the border
> killings. In Texas news, the
> Congressman still has not
> announced whether or not he
> will seek re-election...

Half of Dennis's head is gone. Dennis groans and whimpers piteously when he sees Jace.

Jace is horrified, but determined.

EXT. DALLAS:DENNIS'S APARTMENT BUILDING - NIGHT

Beneath the sound of fireworks, a quieter shot is heard.

INT. DALLAS:DENNIS'S APARTMENT - NIGHT

Jace places Dennis's gun back in his hand.

Jace hears a sound behind him.

He draws his weapon, wheels around and sees Davey crouched in the corner.

INT. DALLAS:DENNIS'S APARTMENT - NIGHT

Davey's face is a frozen mask streaked with blood.

She looks from Jace to Dennis.

Jace and Davey stare at each other for an eternity.

Jace has flecks of Dennis's blood on his face and smears on his hands.

Davey looks at the gun in Jace's hand.

A long moment passes before Jace holsters his weapon and holds out his hand.

> JACE
> Davey. We're not over until
> you say we're over.

Davey takes his hand.

Jace yanks Davey into a hard embrace.

Davey breaks down crying.

Jace wipes her tears away.

Davey pulls away.

                        DAVEY
              We're done here.

Jace holds his breath.

                        DAVEY
              Let's go.

Davey and Jace leave the apartment hand-in-hand.

EXT. DALLAS:DENNIS'S APARTMENT - NIGHT

Fireworks.

FADE OUT
THE END

Screenplay 4

Pretty Diamonds and Rubies

CAST OF CHARACTERS

Jalissa Malton - Black American, female, mid 40s to mid 50s

Lina (voice only) - female, mid 20s to mid 30s

Betty (voice only) - female, mid 40s to mid 50s

Jalissa's Boss (voice only) - male, mid 40s to mid 50s

News Reader (voice only)

Jonathan (voice only) - male, mid 50s

Time
Present day.

FADE IN

INT. STUDIO APARTMENT - DAY

Inside a small, cluttered apartment, the television is on.

A cell phone ringing.

An alarm is blaring.

An empty liquor bottle lays on its side on the floor.

Cigarette butts and ash fill an ash tray.

A hand with a burnt out cigarette butt hovers over a half-empty glass of clear liquid on a table.

Also on the table are a remote control and the ringing cell phone.

Sounds of snoring.

The hand holding the cigarette butt belongs to a disheveled middle-aged Black woman.

She wears a dirty, crumpled work uniform with JALISSA MALTON on the name tag.

The woman wakes up cursing and wipes the hand with the cigarette across her mouth.

                    JALISSA
          What motherfucker?

Jalissa drops the butt, picks up the glass, and drinks the rest down.

                    JALISSA (groaning)
          Goddamnit shut up!

She slams her hand on the alarm, sees the time is 2:15 pm.

                    JALISSA
          Aw, shit! Supposed to wake me
          up at fucking TWO!

Jalissa looks at the television.

                    NEWS READER (voice)
          Traffic on the expressway is
          backed   up   due   to   a
          collision...

                    JALISSA
          The hell ya'll talking about
          now?

                    NEWS READER (voice)
          So please drive carefully on
          your way to the weekend...

Jalissa turns off the television and picks up her cell
phone which indicates three voicemails.

                    JALISSA
          People wait till I'm goddamn
          asleep to call. *Knowing* I work
          nights. Shit.

Jalissa puts her cell phone on speaker and listens to
voice mails while she undresses and takes a clean uniform
out of the closet.

The camera finds a photo of a woman (not Jalissa), a man,
and a young girl.

                    LINA (voice)
          Mama, I just wanted to let you
          know that I took Aunt Betty up
          on her offer to let me stay
          with her in Rollins until I
          can get my beauty salon up and
          running. Uncle Jonathan said
          he would invest some capital.
          And Cousin Kenzi said I could
          stay with her on the weekends.
          (pause) Mama, I think you know
          why I decided to leave town.

Jalissa glares in the direction of the cell phone.

The camera finds a photo of Jalissa and a young girl.

                    LINA (voice)
          It's best for both of us to
          have a little distance from
          each other. I can't deal with
          your problems anymore. I'm
          sorry.

                    JALISSA
          Yeah right.

                    LINA (voice)
          I'm building a new life.
          Anyway, I'm going to be okay.
          I hope you take steps to get
          well too.

Jalissa takes the cell phone into the bathroom and brushes
her teeth.

Toothpaste foam flies everywhere as...

                    JALISSA
        (mimicking Lina) I hope you
        take steps to get well too.
        Siddity-ass. I'm the one that
        raised you! And I didn't
        raise you to be stuck up
        either. Fuck! Now you gonna
        run off even though *I'm* the
        one that put you through
        beauty school in the first
        damn place. Yeah. Okay.
        Ungrateful self ain't *never*
        been worth but a damn. Go on
        then and leave, Lina! Leave
        me be. Just like everybody
        else.

Jalissa spits and clicks a button for the next message.

                    JALISSA
        Who's fucking next?

Jalissa turns on the shower and steps in.

                    JALISSA'S BOSS (voice)
        Ms. Malton, I'm calling to re-
        emphasize what we spoke about
        yesterday. You must arrive to
        work on time from now on and
        then practice a good work
        ethic when you get here. No
        more fighting and arguing. No
        more insubordination. This is
        your last warning. Be on time
        today, behave yourself when
        you get here, or don't bother
        to show up. This is your last
        warning.

                    JALISSA
          Please. Ain't nobody worried
          about that minimum wage
          bullshit. I'll be there when I
          get there. And that's *your*
          last warning!

Jalissa shuts off the shower, steps out, dries off, hits
the button for the next message.

                    BETTY (voice)
          Jalissa, its Betty. Lina's
          with me. I'm not sure what
          happened between you and
          her...

                    JALISSA
          None of your damn judgmental
          business, Betty. Okay? Thank
          you! Lina's *my* child. Too damn
          nosy all the time.

Jalissa struggles into her work uniform.

                    BETTY (voice)
          You're my sister and Lina's
          my niece so you know I'll
          take care of her. Jonathan
          and Kenzi will help out too.
          We'll get everything squared
          away and I know Lina will
          want you to be the first
          customer to get your hair
          done at her salon.

Jalissa stuffs her uncombed unruly hair under her work
hat.

                    JALISSA
          Bitch   please.   Lina   ain't
          touching   my   hair.   So
          whatever.   Your   ex-husband
          just   better   have   my   check
          ready.   Okay?   Else   your
          jealous   ass   is   gonna   find   out
          the *real* reason   he's   helping
          Lina   with   the   salon.

Jalissa laughs and looks at the framed photo of Betty,
Jonathan, and Kenzi.

Then Jalissa looks at the framed photo of her and Lina.

                    JALISSA
          One   big   happy   hypocrite
          family.   That   motherfucker's
          late   with   my   check.   He *better*
          get   my   money   up   here.   I   got
          lights   to   keep   on.

INT/EXT. STUDIO APARTMENT - DAY

Jalissa totally misses the eviction notice on her
apartment door.

INT/EXT. CAR - DAY

Jalissa's car is in disrepair--broken headlight, dings,
scratches.

Jalissa drives past her liquor store.

Jalissa honks her horn and yells out of the car window at
someone she knows.

                    JALISSA
          Damn, that line is too long.
          Can't even get a taste before
          I go in to work to settle my
          damn nerves down. Everybody
          just keeps on *fucking* with me
          today! Wait a minute.

Jalissa takes off her seat belt to feel under the car
seat.

                    JALISSA
          I know that fucker better
          still be here...

Jalissa pulls out a bottle with two fingers of clear
liquid.

                    JALISSA
          Gotcha!

Jalissa takes a swig.

                    JALISSA
          Finally. Now I can fucking
          think.

Jalissa yells out of the window at someone who honks at
her.

                    JALISSA
          Shit. Fuck Lina. I don't need
          her. I don't need Betty
          either. I'm still young. Soon
          as Jonathan sends me my
          money, I'm gonna buy me some
          diamonds and rubies and wear
          them to the club. I'll treat
          my damn-self right if nobody
          else will. Fuck THAT! Don't
          ya'll fucking judge me! Do.
          Not. Fucking. Judge. Me. Just
          a little more time and I'll
          be back on my feet. All I
          need is a little more time.
          So get off my back!

Jalissa digs around the car seat and finds a cigarette in
a crevice.

                    JALISSA
          Good enough! Shit.

Jalissa lights the cigarette and looks at the car's clock
radio.

                    JALISSA
          Aw damn, I'm about to be
          late!

Jalissa presses the accelerator and screams out of the
window at a driver who honks at her.

                    JALISSA
          Jonathan, you better have my
          money, you mangy bastard. Oh,
          I'll sang it, honey. I'll sang
          to the whole world who Lina's
          real daddy is! Shoulda thought
          about that BEFORE you got
          married to my sister, nasty
          motherfucker! Better have my
          money right, I know *that!* Buy
          me some diamonds and rubies
          with that bullshit and wear
          them motherfuckers to the
          grocery store!

Still on speaker, Jalissa's cell phone rings to voicemail.

Jalissa screams out of the window at a passing car.

                    JALISSA' BOSS (voice)
          Ms. Malton, I am looking at
          the clock right now and
          watching the front door. As of
          yet, you are nowhere in sight.
          You have five minutes to
          arrive, Ms. Malton. Otherwise,
          don't bother.

                    JALISSA
          NeverMIND, motherfucker! I'm
          gonna get paid regardless.
          Okay?

Jalissa laughs and sings *diamonds and rubies* to herself.

                    JALISSA (laughing)
          Song's supposed to be
          diamonds and *rubies*. Not
          diamonds and pearls.

Jalissa looks at other drivers with scorn and disgust.

>   JALISSA
>   Look at these non-driving-ass
>   fools! Nobody gives a good
>   goddamn anymore. He's on his
>   cell phone. That one just
>   drove through construction.
>   Tailgating. That bitch is
>   putting makeup on her ugly-ass
>   face. (yelling) It ain't gonna
>   help you, bitch! That one's
>   shoving Burger King up his
>   nose. People on their cell
>   phones. Oh, I *hate* this place!

Jalissa honks her car horn and curses out the car window.

Jalissa's cell phone rings again.

>   JALISSA
>   I ain't THAT late. Damn! Sick
>   of this workplace harassment
>   fool stalking me. Gonna
>   report him.

>   JONATHAN (voice)
>   Jalissa, I claimed Lina as my
>   daughter today. Just now. I
>   told Lina and Betty and Kenzi
>   what I should have told them
>   years ago. I've apologized to
>   everyone. And now I'm going to
>   apologize to you too because
>   you deserved better.

Jalissa narrows her eyes.

                    JONATHAN (voice)
          Anyway, rather than sending
          payment to you for keeping
          secret what should never have
          been secret, I'm going to
          invest in Lina's small
          business. I believe in her.
          That's why I sent money to put
          her through school. Jalissa,
          there won't be a check for you
          anymore, but we have a
          daughter that we can both feel
          proud of.

Jalissa's face is blank.

A car horn blares.

Jalissa swerves, then screams.

Her car crumples on impact.

Shards of windshield glass glitter as they rain down upon
Jalissa.

Jalissa bleeds from her nose, mouth, and ears onto the
steering wheel.

She stirs and groans, then lays across the seat.

Tears leak from her eyes.

Piles of broken glass glitter on the seat. Some of the
glass turns red and shiny.

                    JALISSA (whispering)
          Pretty diamonds and rubies.

Jalissa smiles and closes her eyes.

FADE OUT
THE END

Screenplay 5

You Have to Pay the Cost to be the Boss

CAST OF CHARACTERS

DISTINGUISED MAN/HOMELESS MAN - Black, male, mid 30s to mid 50s

HIGH-CLASS HOOKER/LOW-CLASS HOOKER - female 20s to 30s

TIME
Present day.

FADE IN

INT. CONDO - DAY

DISTINGUISHED MAN wakes up in a four-poster bed.

He showers.

In front of a mirror, he buttons a shirt, puts on a jacket, and straightens his tie.

He smiles with confidence.

He sits down to a nicely-laid table with an expensive breakfast.

INT. CONDEMNDED BUILDING - DAY

HOMELESS MAN wakes up inside a torn, dirty sleeping bag on top of a layer of cardboard, on top of concrete.

He rolls over into a rain leak.

He uses his shirt tail to wipe the rain off his face, ruffles through minimal possessions, and slings a backpack over his shoulder.

He eats a candy bar.

INT. COFFEE SHOP - DAY

Distinguished Man smiles and carries a foamy coffee concoction and a pastry to a chair.

He pulls out a small notebook and taps on the keyboard.

EXT. COFFEE SHOP - DAY

Homeless Man digs around in a garbage can.

He pulls out a paper coffee cup.

He sits the coffee cup on a patio table in front of him.

INT. OFFICE BUILDING - DAY

Distinguished Man sits in a sleek, upscale office.

He tracks stock prices on print outs and a computer screen, then executes transactions.

EXT. VACANT LOT - DAY

Homeless Man scratches off a lottery ticket.

He doesn't win.

INT. RESTAURANT - NIGHT

Distinguished Man sits at a table with cloth napkins, multiple silverware, and wine glasses.

He hands a menu back to the waiter who bows.

INT. SOUP KITCHEN - NIGHT

Homeless Man holds out a tray.

Someone uses an ice cream scoop to drop macaroni and cheese onto his tray.

INT. ART GALLERY - NIGHT

Distinguished Man stands in front of a painting, sipping a glass of wine.

EXT. ALLEY - NIGHT

Homeless Man pees on a graffiti wall with one hand, sipping beer out of a paper bag with the other.

INT. CONDO - NIGHT

Distinguished Man watches sports on flat screen television.

He plays video games.

EXT. SPORTS BAR - NIGHT

Homeless Man watches television through the alley window.

He throws dice.

INT. CONDO - DAY

Distinguished Man runs on a treadmill in his home gym.

Then he gets on a stair climber.

EXT. STREET - DAY

Homeless Man runs behind garbage cans to avoid police.

He throws handfuls of bread crumbs into the air.

Pigeons swarm the police chasing him.

INT. PASSENGER TRAIN - DAY

Distinguished man enjoys the view from the window of a private sleeper car.

EXT. FREIGHT TRAIN - DAY

Homeless man grasps the edge of a box car and heaves himself over the side.

INT. CABIN - NIGHT

Distinguished man opens the door to a luxurious cabin and smiles.

EXT. FOREST - NIGHT

Homeless Man shivers inside his sleeping bag and slaps at mosquitoes.

INT. CABIN - DAY

Distinguished Man cooks fish over the fire.

EXT. FOREST - DAY

Homeless Man chases a goose through a city park.

EXT. VACANT LOT - DAY

Distinguished Man wears a volunteer t-shirt.

He picks up cans and other trash and separates them into recycle bins.

EXT. VACANT LOT - DAY

Homeless Man picks cans and bottles out of the trash and recycle bins.

He crushes them and puts them into a garbage bag.

INT. PRIVATE CLUB - DAY

Distinguished Man points and grins from the stage as he auctions himself off for charity.

EXT. CLINIC - DAY

Homeless Man sells semen and blood.

INT. CONDO - NIGHT

Distinguished Man enjoys the rapt attention of HIGH-CLASS HOOKER.

                    DISTINGUISHED MAN
          I'm gonna need you all night.

                    HIGH-CLASS HOOKER
          I'll take you all around the
          world, baby. But it'll cost
          you.

Distinguished Man throws a handful of bills at High-Class Hooker who squeals and laughs.

INT. CONDEMNED BUILDING - NIGHT

Against a wall, Homeless Man holds a LOW-CLASS HOOKER close.

                    HOMELESS MAN (coughing)
          I love you. You can stay with
          me if you like. I can take
          care of you.

Low-Class Hooker pushes Homeless Man away and laughs and laughs and laughs at his "home" and his clothing.

                    LOW-CLASS HOOKER
          You have to pay the cost to
          be the boss, baby.

Low-Class Hooker snatches bills out of Homeless Man's
pocket.

She takes another contemptuous look around and leaves.

Homeless Man slumps to the floor, used, alone, and lonely.

EXT. VACANT LOT - DAY

Homeless Man sits on a crate staring around.

Low-Class Hooker's laughter echoes in his head.

He spots a news magazine with an ad for a drug trial in
need of subjects. He circles the ad.

INT. CLINIC - NIGHT

Hooked up to electrodes, Homeless Man's face twitches.

His eyes blink.

EXT. PARK - DAY

Homeless Man walks a dog.

INT. CLINIC - DAY

Homeless Man sells more blood and semen.

INT. SINGLE ROOM APARTMENT - DAY

Homeless Man enters a tiny single room apartment. He
smiles and drops his backpack on a chair.

EXT. STREET - DAY

Homeless Man wears a sandwich board and rings a bell.

EXT. STREET - DAY

Homeless Man rakes leaves.

INT. CLASSROOM - DAY

Homeless Man packs his books into a backpack in a community college classroom.

EXT. STREET - DAY

Homeless Man wears a mascot costume to advertise a restaurant.

EXT. STREET - DAY

Homeless Man sweeps a driveway and sidewalk.

INT. ONE BEDROOM APARTMENT - DAY

Homeless Man enters the front door with a new suitcase and a pleased smile.

He puts the suitcase down by the door.

He walks into the kitchen opening the refrigerator door and microwave.

He throws his head back and laughs.

INT. TELEMARKETING BOILER ROOM - DAY

Between calls, Homeless Man circles additional calls for
science experiment subjects in a newspaper.

INT. CLINIC - DAY

Hooked up to monitors, Homeless Man twitches and blinks.

INT. BARBERSHOP - DAY

Homeless Man pays for a thorough grooming.

Transformed into Distinguished Man, he leaves a healthy
tip.

INT. OFFICE - DAY

Distinguished Man stands and shakes hands with someone
across the desk.

INT. MENSWEAR SHOP - DAY

Distinguished Man gets measured by a tailor.

He lowers his shirt tail over the scar where one kidney
used to be.

INT. CONDO - DAY

Distinguished Man enters the condo with the white four-
poster bed with sunglasses, a confident smile, and
matching luggage.

Distinguished Man sits to eat a fine breakfast.

His cufflinks sparkle.

He can't hold the fork because his hand is shaky.

Distinguished Man frowns at his hand.

Next to his glass of juice is a cocktail of medication.

His shaky hand reaches out towards either one.

FADE OUT
THE END

Screenplay 6

Celara Electric

CAST OF CHARACTERS

Martina (Marti) Butler - female, Black, mid-30s

Alexander (Alex) King - male, mid-40s

Evan Lewis - male, early 30s

TIME

Present day.

FADE IN

INT. ALEX KING'S GARAGE - NIGHT

A man (ALEXANDER/ALEX KING) in a three-piece suit gets
into the driver's side of an expensive sedan. A woman
(MARTINA/MARTI BUTLER) in a red cocktail dress gets into
the passenger seat.

                    MARTI
          Did anyone say anything about
          you leaving your own party
          early? Are they gonna ask
          where we went?

                    ALEX
          I just told them I got lucky.

Marti gasps. Alex starts the engine and clicks to open the
garage door.

                    ALEX (laughs)
          No, Marti. No.

Alex turns on the car's heater and backs the car down the
driveway.

                    ALEX
          I told them I had to take care
          of something at Celara. They
          know I work around the clock.

EXT. ALEX'S MANSION - NIGHT

The large mansion is ablaze with lights amid sounds of
revelry and music as the garage door closes.

INT. ALEX'S CAR - NIGHT

         ALEX
Besides, after I shook hands
all around and told them to
liquor up, nobody gave a shit
where I was going. My staff
will wrap things up.

         MARTI (laughs)
Brilliant as always, Alex. I
guess that's why you make the
big bucks.

         ALEX (smiling)
Buckle up for safety.

Marti and Alex buckle up. Alex drives down the road.

         ALEX
So where do we go from here?

         MARTI
At the light, hang a right.
Right here.

Alex laughs and turns the corner.

         MARTI
Down this road about ten
miles, over the channel bridge
and then I'm two more blocks
down on the left at Day and
Carter Road. I'll tell you
where to stop.

         ALEX (still laughing)
God, I celebrate the day I
hired you, Marti.

         MARTI
What's so funny?

                    ALEX
I meant 'where do we go from
here' about you and me. After
tonight. But thanks for the
directions.

                    MARTI (laughing)
Oh yeah. That. Well, I guess
it finally happened, hunh?

                    ALEX (muttering)
Yeah. *That.* Took you long
enough.

                    MARTI
Oh stop it.

                    ALEX
Marti, I'm serious. You don't
have to struggle through the
corporate jungle. You're not
by yourself anymore. I'll take
care of you. Make sure
everything's all right.

                    MARTI
No, Alex. I'm okay. I mean,
that's not why I... I mean, I
would never do something like
that. I'm not that type of
girl. I can take care of
myself.

                    ALEX
So I've seen.

                    MARTI
I made it this far without...
you know. Anyway, I'm fine. I
don't need you to take care of
me.

                    ALEX
          I repeat, where do we go from
          here?

                    MARTI
          Well, where do you want to go?

                    EVAN (from the backseat)
          Good question, Marti.

EVAN rises to sitting position in the back seat. Marti
shrieks. Alex swears and pulls over to the side of the
road.

The car engine idles.

                    ALEX
          Evan, what the fuck?

Marti and Alex notice the gun in Evan's hand at the same
time. Marti looks to Alex for direction.

                    ALEX
          Sit still.

                    EVAN
          No Alex. Keep going. We've got
          to get our little Marti safely
          home, don't we? Over the
          channel bridge and then two
          more blocks on the left. Day
          and Carter Road. *I'll* tell you
          where to stop.

With another glance at the gun, Alex pulls back onto the
road.

                    EVAN
          Marti, you know, I hate to see
          you deluded. It really, really
          (pause) really, really causes
          me actual pain to see you
          walking around the office with
          your head in the clouds
          thinking shit doesn't stink.
          Well, shit stinks! Shit stinks
          to high heaven. Especially
          when you wallow in it. Right,
          Boss?

Alex flicks his eyes to the rear view mirror, meets Evan's
gaze.

                    ALEX (neutral voice)
          Sure.

                    EVAN
          There's a way to get things
          done in Lake City. It just
          doesn't happen by writing
          press releases, sister. It
          takes way more than that.

Marti waits.

                    EVAN
          Palms get greased, favors
          owed, threats made, bids
          rigged, projects sabotaged,
          inspections forced, code
          violations overlooked. And
          that, *little girl*, is how it
          works. *That's* how things get
          done in the city. Right, Alex?

                    ALEX (sighs)
          Right, Evan.

                    EVAN
          Tell her about Lakeside.

                    ALEX
          That's confidential.

                    EVAN
          Tell her, Alex. She needs to
          get things straight in her
          head. She needs to know how
          we do it at Celara. Go
          ahead, Boss. Tell her
          everything about Lakeside.

Alex glances at the gun, then keeps his eyes focused
forward.

                    ALEX
          Celara would take over the
          Lakeside contract and retro-
          convert it not only to
          photovoltaic, but also to
          solar thermal. Then purchase
          majority ownership. Our guy
          kept track of the bidding.
          After we approached him, he
          requested a commitment, a show
          of confidence in his business
          plan for retail. I agreed to
          review the business plan and
          an investment.

Marti closes her eyes.

                    MARTI (low voice)
          That's the business plan that
          you gave me to adapt for
          Celara.

                    EVAN
          But wait. There's more! Tell
          her the rest of it, Alex.

                    ALEX
          You tell her. I'm driving.

                    EVAN (eagerly)
We gave him half up front.
He'd get the other half after
you decided the plan was
workable and after he made a
show of faith.

                    MARTI
That explosion... at Lakeside?

                    EVAN (giggles)
At last, we're here.

                    MARTI
Augie died in that blast. He
was my *friend*. You...

                    EVAN
Accidents happen, Marti.

                    MARTI
Augie was your guy. Wasn't he?

Marti glances at Alex. Alex tightens his lips.

                    EVAN
Circle gets the square! Do you
know, he actually threatened
me? (incredulous) Your *Augie*
told me that he was going to
tell you the full truth about
Alex. (smug) Let me tell you,
he settled back down after we
promised him extra funds. Hell
of a guy. A true friend, hunh
Marti? (hard voice) He had no
honor and he got what he
deserved.

Marti stares straight ahead.

                    EVAN
          So based on that, Marti needs
          to understand what it takes to
          really be part of the team. Am
          I right, Alex?

Alex glances at the rear view mirror.

                    ALEX
          Right.

                    EVAN
          She needs to know there's
          nothing she won't do to prove
          her loyalty.

                    ALEX (hesitates)
          Loyalty is important.

Marti stares at Alex, stunned.

                    EVAN
          You heard him right, Marti.
          And I've already proven myself
          time and again. Right, Alex?

                    ALEX
          You know I count on you to
          hold it all together. I've
          told you that. Time and again.

                    EVAN
          That's right! And anyone not
          on the team gets dealt with
          and that's just the way it is.

Marti cringes.

                    EVAN (sneering)
See? I told you, Alex! She
just doesn't get it. You women
are all the same. (shakes
head) Marti, Marti, Marti. I'm
so sorry the big, bad world
(makes finger quotes) hurt
you. But there's a war going
on in construction, *little
girl*. I'm talking right here
in the city. I'm on the
battlefield *everyday*. And in a
war, sometimes there's
friendly fire. There's
collateral damage. Sacrifice
for the greater good. Some
things cannot be helped, you
know? We all have our
positions to maintain and our
roles to play. You do know
your role now, don't you?

                    MARTI (quiet tone)
What is my role?

                    EVAN
Marti, if Alex wanted
something done, *I made it
happen*. If he wanted something
undone, I made *that* happen. I
do what I have to do. Life is
a battlefield and I am a
soldier. I walk through the
fire for Celara and for Alex.
Don't I, Alex! While the
whiners and complainers talk
about it, I *am* about it. While
you're lecturing and shaking
that prissy little finger of
yours all around, I'm getting
the information and I'm
getting it done.

                    MARTI
What information?

                    EVAN (shakes head)
Marti, oh my God. Come *on*!
We're telecommunications and
electronic surveillance not
just electrical construction.
It's all right there in your
research. *Jesus!* Where've you
been? Hello? Anyone home?

Evan snaps his fingers by Marti's head.

                    EVAN (sniggers)
Honey, quit looking at the
trees and see the forest. We
can follow people wherever
they go. Did he really take
the day off for sick leave, or
did he spend the day at the
strip club? Pharmacy, grocery
store, doctor's office, post
office, library. Prostitutes,
girlfriends, mistresses, and
yeah, sometimes boyfriends
too. Amazing what people will
tell you, show you, *give* you
for, oh, a one hundred dollar
tip. Amazing, but not
surprising in this economy.
Surprising is what you'll find
in their trash cans. God, *the
humanity!* Surprising is what
they'll confess to their
therapists. And not everyone
locks up their credit card
bills. Sometimes, they just
leave them lying out. Full
accounting of every perversion
and twisted tendency.
Leverage, sweetheart. Get to
know it.

                    MARTI
It's   intimidation   and
blackmail.

                    EVAN (interrupts)
Alex, how can you stand it?
Marti, will you please wake up
the fuck up already? You're
making me goddamn tired. Look,
someone's either for us or
against us. It's a choice. And
by the way, you need to decide
which side you're on. Right
now.

Long pause.

                    MARTI
No, I understand, Evan. I do.
I gave you a hard time in the
office because I had to. I had
do it. You see, I had to know.

                    EVAN (narrows his eyes)
Know fucking what?

                    MARTI
What you were made of. I
needed to know that you're a
stand-up guy. I took it to the
limit with you because I don't
like weak links.

                    EVAN
Really.

                    MARTI
Yeah. Really. I pushed you to
see if you were all I
thought... that... I sensed
you could be.

             EVAN (fascinated)
And what did you decide?

             MARTI
That nobody does it better.
Do you know what it does to me
to see you do your thing and
not give a damn what anybody
thinks? It inspires me, Evan.
I always knew you could take
it to the limit. (breathless)
That's hardcore, baby.

             EVAN
Do   you   like   it   hardcore,
Marti?

             MARTI
You mean you didn't know?

             EVAN
You sure fooled me.

             MARTI
That's why I'm so good.

Alex directs a "what the hell are you doing?" look at
Marti. Marti ignores that and smirks at Evan.

             EVAN
Join us, Marti. Between the
three   of   us,   we'd   be
unstoppable. Alex, you, me--
we'd have all angles covered.
Because let's face it.

Marti reacts to Evan's breath crawling up her neck.

             EVAN
With Kate gone, we're missing
a soft touch.

Evan leans closer to Marti.

                    EVAN
          Of course, me and Alex would
          have to take you for a test
          run. Make sure that *you* can
          take it to the limit.

Evan strokes Marti's hair and cheek with the gun.

                    EVAN
          But then... Alex started the
          party without me in the green
          house, didn't he?

Marti closes her eyes.

                    MARTI
          You saw us?

                    EVAN
          Good times. (laughs) I guess
          that's why he's the Boss. But
          Marti, ohhh Marti. (groans
          aloud) I can't wait until it's
          my turn to touch you on the
          inside too.

Marti shudders and shakes her head. She chokes back a
scream.

                    ALEX (angrily)
          Evan...

                    EVAN
          Teach you the ropes. Show you
          how to make a man really beg
          for mercy.

Evan groans again. His lips touch Marti's ear. He holds
the gun in one hand. The other hand touches himself out of
camera range.

                    EVAN (excited)
Oh, my God. A body like yours
was just built for espionage,
babe. Corporate Research...
Director. That's your new
title, sweetie. Director of
Corporate Research and
Business Intelligence. It'll
look good on your resume. And
I just know you could do it.
(cruel) Alex already knows it.
Don't you, Alex? Because once
Marti starts, she never stops.
Gold star for perseverance,
honey.

Alex's fingers tighten then whiten on the steering wheel.

                    EVAN
Tell her what you told me.
Tell her what you used to say
about her.

                    ALEX
Those were just jokes, Evan.

                    EVAN (snickering)
No they weren't.

                    MARTI (exasperated)
Look, I'm in. I'm on the team,
Evan. Let's just... get it
started.

                    EVAN (shouting)
Don't fuck with us, Marti.
Don't you do it, babe. Don't
do it!

Marti stares forward, eyes wide open, too scared to blink.

EXT. DARK ROAD - NIGHT

There are no other cars on the road in front or behind.

Deep snow covers the countryside.

INT. ALEX'S CAR - NIGHT

                    EVAN
          Kate was the last woman who
          fucked with us. Now where is
          she, Marti? Where is Kate?
          Nowhere. Think about that.
          Think real long and hard about
          that. She actually said that I
          could never be the man Alex
          was. Do you know what I did? I
          told her to shut the fuck up
          over and over. But she kept
          talking shit. I tell you what
          (long pause), she didn't say a
          word after I slapped her
          around and then fucked her to
          death.

A sick feeling bubbles up Marti's esophagus.

                    EVAN
          Oh yeah. That's right. Over
          and over I did it to her hard.
          I held her by the neck until
          she stopped breathing.
          (giggles) I didn't even know I
          had that much endurance.
          Marti, how long would you bet
          that I could make you happy?

Marti struggles to keep her composure.

                    ALEX (shocked)
          My God, Evan.

                    EVAN
          Don't worry, Alex. I took care
          of it. Kate tried to play us
          off each other so she had to
          go.

Evan turns toward Marti.

                    EVAN
          And no one's ever going to
          find out. Are they?

Marti stares at darkness through the windshield.

Alex closes his eyes a brief moment then refocuses on the
road.

EXT. CHANNEL BRIDGE - NIGHT

Alex's car lights show in the distance, approaching the
channel bridge.

INT. ALEX'S CAR - NIGHT

                    ALEX
          Evan, you know, there was
          never anything between me and
          Kate. Look, she tried, sure.
          But I held her off because I
          knew you two had something
          going on. She was just fucking
          with your head trying to get
          you to react.

Alex hits the steering wheel with his fist.

                    ALEX (shouts)
          And you let her!

                    EVAN
          Alex. You know… its fine. Kate
          was a bitch.

Evan turns back to Marti.

                    EVAN
          She was a *bitch*, Marti. She
          was a warm piece of moist ass.
          Fuck her. That's all women
          are, Marti. Even *you,* special
          as you are. You do know that's
          all you'll ever be to him...
          and to me? (sneering) Ah yes,
          the greenhouse.

Marti leans her head against the passenger window,
disgusted.

Evan smirks at Marti's humiliation. He glances at Alex.
Alex's frozen expression confuses Evan.

Marti takes a deep breath and holds back revulsion because
she has to convince Evan.

                    MARTI
          Well, she deserved it.

                    EVAN
          The fuck you talking about
          now?

                    MARTI
          Kate. She asked for it.

                    EVAN (silky)
          Right, Marti. Right. (pause)
          Just like your mother asked
          for it?

Marti flinches.

                    MARTI
          What did you say?

                    ALEX
          Evan, don't. Don't do it.

                    EVAN (laughs)
          Come on, Alex. She's tough.
          You tell me that all the time.

                    ALEX
          Don't, Evan. Just stop.

                    EVAN
          Aren't you, Marti? You're
          tough. You sit there just like
          you always do. So cool, calm,
          and collected. *Calculated*.
          Nothing ever rattles that
          icicle cage. Or does it, you
          lovely ice queen? What were
          you *really* up to in that
          greenhouse tonight? What do
          you think, Alex?

Marti turns her head to look at Evan.

Evan stares cold, angry eyes into Marti's. Marti looks
towards Alex's profile.

Alex frowns, shakes his head, but doesn't meet Marti's
gaze.

Marti faces forward again, disappointed. She sees the
channel bridge in the distance.

                    EVAN
          Why do you think your mother
          did it, Marti? Hmmm?

Marti can't breathe.

EXT. CHANNEL BRIDGE - NIGHT

The cold steel of the channel bridge gleams in the headlights.

INT. ALEX'S CAR - NIGHT

          EVAN
    Do you think your mother
    slooowly reasoned out the
    details the same way you do
    and slooowly came to the
    conclusion that your father's
    life was worth five times more
    than that of *a drunken*
    alcoholic slut who couldn't
    even feed her own children or
    clean her own house?

Marti screams. Angry tears start in her eyes.

          ALEX
    Marti no! No!

She twists as far as the seatbelt allows. She reaches to claw Evan's face. To gouge his eyes. To shut his mouth.

Evan bats Marti's hands away with a laugh. Then he backhands her across the left temple with the gun.

Marti's head ricochets right. Stunned, Tears roll down her face, though she doesn't make a sound and she doesn't move.

Evan raises the gun again so Marti can see it.

                    EVAN
          I've had just about enough out
          of you, Martina Butler. Me and
          Alex have completely had it!
          You think you can do my job?
          You think you can do what I
          do? It's me and him in it
          together. You'll never mean
          more to him than me. I've
          walked through the fire for
          Alex!

Evan's voice escalates to a scream.

                    EVAN
          Never! Do you get it, you
          bitch? Never! Do you get it?
          Do you?

Alex yanks the steering wheel hard to the right.

Evan's gunshot breaks Marti's passenger window.

EXT. CHANNEL BRIDGE - NIGHT

The car spins on the ice, hits the guardrail on the left,
then whips across the road head on towards the right
guardrail.

INT. ALEX'S CAR - NIGHT

Evan flies into the windshield on impact and crumples face
down between Marti and Alex.

EXT. CHANNEL BRIDGE - NIGHT

                    MARTI (screaming)
          No! No!

The car tips over the rail.

INT. ALEX'S CAR - NIGHT

Marti screams and screams again.

EXT. CHANNEL BRIDGE - NIGHT

The car skids down ice-covered concrete towards the water.

INT. ALEX'S CAR - NIGHT

                    ALEX
          Marti, get out!

                    MARTI (hysterical)
          No! No!

                    ALEX
          Jump! Do it, Marti! Do it now!

                    MARTI
          I can't!

EXT. CHANNEL BRIDGE - NIGHT

The car hits the water with a large splash.

Fade to black and sounds of gurgling water.

EXT. CHANNEL BRIDGE:EMBANKMENT - NIGHT

Cold steel gleams like prison bars. Ice shifts. Water gurgles.

Marti lays motionless on the channel's concrete embankment.

Alex kneels over Marti, his hands somewhere near her throat.

Marti wakes with a cough and a choke. She retches and cries.

Alex hugs her to his chest.

>   ALEX
> Marti. Oh my God, Marti.

>   MARTI
> Alex? Where's Evan?

Marti follows Alex's glance at the ice. She shivers.

>   ALEX
> He won't hurt you anymore.

>   MARTI
> Is he still down there?

>   ALEX
> It's over now.

Alex kisses Marti.

>   MARTI
> We have to call the police!

>   ALEX
> Wait.

>   MARTI
> Wait? Wait for what? Alex...

Marti sits up. She sees bloody cuts on Alex's hands and arms. His shirt hangs in bloody rags. She sees cuts on her arms and shoulders.

Still exhausted, Marti lays back in Alex's arms.

>   MARTI
> Alex, is it true what Evan
> said about Kate?

There is a silence that is too long.

Marti struggles to her feet.

>   MARTI
>   I'm going home.

Alex helps her up and they struggle up the concrete
embankment towards the road together.

>   ALEX (sighs)
>   Marti, every single damn day
>   of my life, my father kicked
>   my ass and ground me under his
>   heel. I had to earn the
>   privilege of being his son and
>   prove myself worthy. He said,
>   even though I was special and
>   better than everyone else, it
>   was my duty to do whatever it
>   took to protect the family
>   name and the family business.
>   I would have done anything to
>   earn his respect because it
>   didn't come easy. Nothing from
>   him came easy.

Marti closes her eyes in despair.

>   MARTI
>   We have to...

>   ALEX
>   I know that doesn't compare to
>   the heartache you experienced
>   growing up and how you lost
>   your mother. But things can
>   always get better for both of
>   us if we try.

>   MARTI
>   Alex, we can't just... We have
>   to do something about... about
>   Evan.

                ALEX
        Stay with me, Marti. It's
        going to get better, I promise
        you. I'll see to it.

                MARTI (insistent)
        What about *Kate*?

                ALEX (impatient)
        What *about* Kate?

Marti looks at Alex without speaking.

She lets go of Alex's hand as they reach the start of the
bridge.

EXT. CHANNEL BRIDGE:ROAD - NIGHT

Marti and Alex rest for a moment after the long climb.

                ALEX
        I needed her help to keep Evan
        in line. You knew how he could
        be.

Marti looks down at the hole in the ice.

                MARTI
        You used Evan and Kate against
        each other.

Alex shrugs.

                MARTI
        Well, that plan sure worked.

                ALEX
        Not the way I thought it
        would.

                MARTI
        No kidding.

                    ALEX
          Kate knew exactly what she was
          getting into. She knew the
          deal. I told her.

                    MARTI
          But you didn't tell her how
          sick Evan really was. You
          didn't tell her... she might
          die.

                    ALEX
          I don't think even *I* knew how
          fucked in the head he was.

                    MARTI
          I wish I never met him.

Alex looks at Marti.

                    ALEX
          Or me?

Marti looks away and doesn't answer.

                    ALEX
          Marti, I couldn't go against
          him when he had a gun to your
          head!

                    MARTI
          I know that! But what about
          Augie?

Marti and Alex begin the slow walk across the channel
bridge.

                    ALEX
          What?

                    MARTI
          You tried to use me against
          him, just like you used Evan
          against Kate, didn't you?

                    ALEX
          Look, I just needed the bid
          data for Lakeside. That's all
          I wanted. He would give me the
          data once you finished the
          business plan. That was the
          deal. That's it.

Marti stops walking to stare at Alex.

                    MARTI
          Did you know what would happen
          to him at Lakeside? Did you
          know he wouldn't walk away
          from the plant alive?

Alex sighs.

                    MARTI (whispering)
          Did you know?

Silence.

Marti closes her eyes, chokes back tears, and shivers from
cold.

                    MARTI
          First Augie. Then Kate.

Alex shakes his head and puts his arm around Marti.

She shrugs him off.

                    ALEX
          Marti, listen.

                    MARTI
          Now Evan. Who's next?

                    ALEX
          I've been crazy since you left
          me.

                    MARTI
          Left you?

                    ALEX
          I don't know if you missed me,
          but I missed you while you
          were gone.

Marti sighs and starts walking.

Alex keeps pace.

                    ALEX
          I know you've got your own
          issues to deal with and
          whatever I've contributed to
          the pain, I'm sorry for that.
          But the way you tossed me
          aside like I didn't even
          matter and... just took
          off...

                    MARTI
          I didn't toss you aside,
          Alex. I resigned my position.
          People do that sometimes, you
          know.

                    ALEX
          Look, I know things are
          complicated, but you're
          important to me, Marti. I
          want you in my life. I would
          do anything to make that
          happen.

Marti looks down at the hole in the ice.

                    ALEX
          Look, I didn't want to tell
          you all of this. I wanted to
          allow you your peace while you
          took some time off.

                    MARTI
          Again, Alex, I didn't take
          time off. I quit! You
          persuaded me back for this
          last project and... (looks
          away) people died.

                    ALEX
          I am not ashamed of how I feel
          for you. I would tell the
          entire world.

                    MARTI
          You're not listening to me.
          One and done. We're through!

Alex reaches for her hand. Marti snatches her hand away.

                    MARTI
          No!

Mental and physical exhaustion slow Marti's steps to small
jerks and drags.

                    ALEX
          Marti… Marti…

Marti shakes her head and takes two more steps away from
Alex.

                    ALEX
          Martina!

Marti pauses.

                    ALEX
          We're not done here!

Marti takes another step.

                    ALEX
          So this is how you deal with
          it? Are you fucking kidding
          me? This is what I hired? When
          the going gets tough, Marti
          runs away. Is that it? That's
          how Marti deals? (outraged
          shout) Goddamnit, *Martina
          Butler!*

Marti looks over her shoulder.

                    ALEX
          You are still on the clock,
          Martina. (shouting) *Get back
          here!*

Marti turns to stare at Alex in total disbelief.

                    ALEX
          I am fucking talking to you,
          Martina. Don't you damn well
          turn your back on me!

                    MARTI (shrieking)
          What Alex? What! What!

Alex takes a breath to speak.

                    MARTI (shrieking)
          What!

Three quarters across, the steel of the channel bridge
frames Martina and Alex inside a metaphorical prison.

                    ALEX (lowers voice)
Marti, you told me that you
would leave several times. But
I thought you would change
your mind if I could pass all
of your (pause) tests. Look,
we have something great going.
I felt it in the greenhouse
tonight and you felt it too. I
know you did. I wasn't alone
in there.

                    MARTI (wearily)
Alex, what is that *noise* that
keeps coming out of your face?

                    ALEX
Look, I'm just not sure what
to say any more because it
seems like lately, I make all
the wrong choices when it
comes to you. I will say this.
Our time together tonight was
so beautiful. It's never been
that good for me with anyone
else. I know that I can make
you happy ever after. If you
stay and continue work at
Celara, we can make each other
happy.

                    MARTI
Continue work at Celara?

Alex nods.

                    MARTI (closes eyes)
Oh my God, I wondered about
the reasons for tonight. But I
wasn't sure until just this
moment.

                    ALEX
          No. Not like that.

                    MARTI
          Evan was right about you.

                    ALEX
          Evan (pause) was a sociopath.

                    MARTI
          He was crazy, but he told me
          the truth. And now he's gone.
          (in wonder) Everyone's gone.

                    ALEX
          Marti, it's you. It was always
          you. You're the one that I
          need.

Marti steps back towards Alex.

                    MARTI
          Alex, do you understand what
          just happened here tonight?
          (shouts) A man is dead!

                    ALEX
          Marti, calm down.

Marti crosses her arms.

                    MARTI (cold voice)
          By the way, I never told you
          how my mother died. I never
          told anyone at Celara. So how
          did you find that out? How did
          Evan know?

Alex doesn't answer.

                    MARTI (swallowing)
          You acquired a great deal of
          personal information about me,
          Alex.   You   shared   that
          information with Evan and God
          only knows who else.

Alex doesn't speak for a long time.

                    ALEX
          It's   just   business,   Marti.
          That's all it is. It's nothing
          more than that.

                    MARTI
          And you would do anything for
          Celara.   Yes,   I   remember.
          That's plenty.

Alex doesn't answer.

                    MARTI
          My entire tenure with you was
          just one big mind fuck. Wasn't
          it?

                    ALEX
          Don't say that.

                    MARTI
          It's already been said. And,
          as of yet, it hasn't been
          denied.

Alex shakes his head.

                    MARTI
          Even on the brink of death,
          even after…

Marti gestures down towards the ice.

                    MARTI
          …not ten minutes ago, you're
          still the same. You use people
          and throw them away when you
          don't need them anymore. I
          understand it all now.

Alex tries to protest.

Marti overrides him with a voice that slices like a
switchblade.

                    MARTI
          What about me, Alex? What *ever*
          are you going to do?

                    ALEX
          Marti, I didn't do that to
          Evan. You were there for the
          whole ride. He was going to
          kill you.

Marti points an accusing finger at Alex.

                    MARTI
          Because you never get your
          hands dirty, Alex. Other
          people do that for you. Did
          Evan know that you meant for
          me to take his place? Is that
          what sent him over the edge?

                    ALEX
          Marti, aren't you being a just
          little melodramatic?

                    MARTI
          Someone just died. (points to
          the ice) He's there! Do you
          see him? He's down there! We…

                    ALEX
          What the hell do you take me
          for?

                MARTI
          If I stay with you, Alex...
          someday that will be me. Won't
          it?

Side-by-side, Alex and Marti stare at the ice and water,
framed by cold steel.

Marti looks nauseated.

                MARTI
          Oh my, God.

                ALEX
          Marti, it's fucking cold and
          we're fucking freezing to
          death out here.

                MARTI (giggling)
          I always did admire your
          confidence, Alex.

                ALEX
          We still have a chance
          together. I can take you
          places, Marti. Help you out
          when you need a friend.

                MARTI
          Hell, face it. The swagger
          totally turned me on.

                ALEX (smiling)
          You and me, Marti. Two against
          the city. It's still not too
          late.

                MARTI
          Who are you really?

Marti looks into Alex's eyes. She turns away in fright
from what she sees (or doesn't see).

                    ALEX
          Don't let Evan win, Marti. Not
          now.

                    MARTI
          He hasn't won. Neither have I.
          And you certainly haven't.

Marti turns her back on Alex and starts to walk away in
jerks and slides.

She's almost off the bridge.

                    ALEX
          Marti, don't do this.

Back still turned, Marti stops walking.

                    MARTI
          What are you going to do,
          Alex?

A long pause.

                    ALEX (slow smile)
          I'll think of something.

A short pause.

Marti looks over her shoulder.

                    MARTI
          I'll be waiting.

Marti walks off the bridge into darkness.

FADE OUT
THE END

Screenplay 7

King of the City

CAST OF CHARACTERS

Tolly Henry - Black, female, mid 30s

Alex King - male, mid 40s

Celara King - female, mid 60s

TIME
Present day.

FADE IN

EXT. OFFICE BUILDING - DAY

On Sunday morning, TOLLY HENRY stands in front of a small camera mounted on a tripod in front of deserted, glass-covered office building in the suburbs.

> TOLLY
> Early this morning, I visited with Alexander King, business man and leader in the green revolution, at his far north suburban headquarters of Celara Wind to discuss his mayoral campaign. His wife and children joined us for the interview...

Profanity erupts over TOLLY'S shoulder.

She sighs and resets the camera to record.

> TOLLY
> This camera picks up *everything*.

This time, she hears screams.

Tolly turns to see ALEX KING strike someone and yank their arm.

She hears children crying.

Alex shouts more expletives and gestures wildly.

He draws his right hand back to his left shoulder for a backhand hit.

Hand still raised for the hit, Alex glances up.

He sees Tolly and her camera watching him.

                    ALEX (shouting)
        What the fuck?

Alex stalks across the parking lot

He reaches past Tolly to grab the camera.

Tolly backs away, knocking the camera and tripod to the
asphalt behind her.

She looks around for help. There's no one to help her.

                    ALEX
        What are you trying to do
        here, Tolly?

He stands so close that he breathes Tolly's air.

                    ALEX
        You realize you can't leave
        here with that footage, don't
        you?

Tolly takes a step back. Alex takes a step forward.

                    ALEX
        You filmed a private moment
        between me and my family. I
        gave you a good interview and
        permission   to   film   my
        building. That's it. This
        issn't part of the deal. You
        know what I want. Put it in my
        hand. Right now.

Alex holds out his hand.

                    TOLLY
        I can't do that, Alex. I need
        the camera for work. They'll
        take it out of my check.
        I'll… I'll… edit the part…

                    ALEX
          Deal's off. Give me that
          camera, or watch me take it
          from you.

Alex takes another step towards Tolly.

Tolly's blocked in a corner.

                    TOLLY
          Alex, please. Don't do this.
          I'll take care of it. I won't…

Alex yanks Tolly forward by the arm.

He shakes her like a rag doll until her teeth snap
together.

                    TOLLY
          Stop it! Don't! Don't!

Tolly struggles to pull her arm away.

                    ALEX
          Oh no you don't!

Alex tries to push past Tolly to get to the camera on the
ground.

                    ALEX
          Give it to me!

Tolly blocks Alex with her body.

He grabs her by the arm again.

                    TOLLY
          No! You're hurting me!

                    ALEX
          I've come too far.

> TOLLY
> Stop it, Alex!

Tolly shoves Alex away. She dives to pick up the camera and tripod.

> ALEX
> Bitch!

Alex grabs Tolly shirt tail and rips it.

> ALEX
> Get back here!

> TOLLY
> Let go of me!

Tolly strikes at Alex's hands.

Over the sound of children screaming, Tolly hears a car door slam shut.

> CELARA (voice)
> What is going on here?

Alex releases his hold on Tolly's shirt.

Snorting like a dragon, he turns to face the newcomer.

CELARA, a regal mid 60s woman with brunette hair accented by a silver streak faces Alex and Tolly.

Her tailored navy suit, leather shoes, and violet-tinged designer sunglasses scream money.

Tolly struggles not to cry in relief.

She attempts to slow her breathing.

> CELARA
> I've seen enough. I think you
> should leave. Now.

Tolly starts to move, but to Tolly's surprise, it's Alex

who walks back across the parking lot without a word. Along the way, he smooths his tailored suit and hair in place.

He shoves his family into the car.

He gives Tolly one last glare before he gets into the driver's seat.

>   CELARA
> Miss, you seem terribly upset.

>   TOLLY (trembling voice)
> I am.

>   CELARA
> Can I call someone for you?

>   TOLLY
> No. There's… no one to call, really.

>   CELARA
> Would you like a ride home?

Alex drives away.

>   TOLLY
> I guess I'd better get a ride. I'm not up to walking to the bus stop by myself. And I don't know if he'll circle the building to try to find me alone again.

>   CELARA
> I completely understand.

>   TOLLY
> Just let me get my shoulder bag.

In a few shaky steps, Tolly retrieves the bag, and shoves the camera, tripod, and notebook inside.

She turns and let out a squeak because the woman hovers over her.

>   CELARA
>   Ready?

They cross the empty parking lot to an expensive sedan parked on the street.

>   TOLLY
>   I just can't believe that
>   actually happened in broad
>   daylight. I didn't expect it.
>   It came out of nowhere.

The woman unlocks the car doors with a flick of her key ring.

>   CELARA
>   Things like that don't come
>   out of nowhere. What set him
>   off?

INT/EXT. CAR:SUBURBS - DAY

They get in the car.

>   TOLLY
>   I think it was the kids. They
>   were crying during his
>   interview.

>   CELARA
>   I guess that would do it.

>   TOLLY (frowning)
>   It's still not right. Alex
>   King is a bad man.

The woman's smile disappears.

                    TOLLY
          A very bad, angry man.

No answer.

                    TOLLY
          You saw him.

                    CELARA
          I certainly saw something.
          Which way are we going, ah…

                    TOLLY
          Tolly. Henry.

                    CELARA
          Tolly Henry. So. Am I taking
          you home?

                    TOLLY
          Oh. Yes. If you would.

Tolly shakes her head.

                    TOLLY
          Sorry. I'm still a little
          rattled. I'm in a three-flat
          at 15th and Cherry Road.

INT/EXT. CAR:CITY - DAY

The sedan cuts through city traffic like a gunboat through
water.

                    CELARA
          Are you by yourself?

                    TOLLY
          You mean? Yes, I'm single.

The woman nods.

                    TOLLY
          I'm on the basement level.
          Over there.

INT/EXT. CAR:CITY:THREE-FLAT - DAY

Tolly points out the clean, but worn down three-story
structure.

                    TOLLY
          I manage that building. Well,
          mostly, I keep things afloat.

                    CELARA
          That's wonderful to be so
          independent.

                    TOLLY
          I   suppose.   Building
          management's a lot of work,
          but I like it.

                    CELARA
          Sometimes independence can be
          a problem.

                    TOLLY
          I guess.

                    CELARA
          Most powerful men will stop
          at nothing to get what they
          want, when they want it.

The woman pulls to the curb in front of Tolly's building.

                    TOLLY (laughs)
          Trust me, I know.

                    CELARA
          Whatever it takes.

Tolly blinks.

> CELARA
> I mean, do you have a way to
> defend yourself if things
> become difficult?

An awkward pause.

> TOLLY
> Difficult with Alex King?

> CELARA
> He seemed to really want
> whatever it was that you
> didn't give him. Was it the
> camera that you put inside
> your bag?

Tolly senses something's not right.

> TOLLY
> You weren't just passing by
> this morning, were you?

> CELARA
> Maybe, just to make life
> easier, you should give him
> whatever it is that he wants
> rather than make him take it
> from you.

The woman removes her sunglasses.

Tolly follows the woman's line of vision towards the address clearly marked on her building.

> TOLLY
> Maybe.

> CELARA
> Oh, there's lots of maybes in
> life. Maybe he knows where you
> live. Alone.

The woman's eyes slide across the building's worn facade.

                    CELARA
          Maybe he knows that you are…
          financially vulnerable.

Tolly looks embarrassed.

The building's exterior is clean and swept, but still in
need of renovation.

The woman's smile returns.

                    CELARA
          There's lots of maybes in
          life.

                    TOLLY
          Who are you?

                    CELARA
          Celara.

                    TOLLY
          That's the name of his
          company.

                    CELARA
          And the name of his mother.

The woman sticks out a hand, manicured, rings on several
fingers, expensive watch.

                    CELARA
          Celara King. Pleased to meet
          you, Tolly Henry.

Tolly reaches for the passenger door handle.

Click.

Celara King engages the child safety lock.

CELARA
I'm very sure things will work
out for my son in the primary,
Tolly. And maybe things will
work out for you and your
building. But maybe they
won't. And, in anticipation of
the maybes in life, we have
many relationships and many
resources in Lake City.

TOLLY
Alex won't get away with what
he did to me or his wife.
He'll never make it through
the primary if people learn
what he really is.

CELARA
People tell us that, but we're
still here. I'm sure just like
a good little *reporter,* as you
call yourself, you researched
Alex prior to your interview
with him?

TOLLY
Of course, I did.

CELARA (smiling)
Of course you did. So you've
probably already discovered
that the police union supports
his campaign. He's certainly
been supportive of their
causes. Whereas the campaign
of that… *Yashuda woman.*

TOLLY
Tina Yashuda.

                    CELARA
Whatever. Lie after lie after
lie, Tolly. That's all
Yashuda's got. She's
desperate. She has reason to
be desperate because she has
nothing to offer this city and
the voters know that.

                    TOLLY
What about the lies to cover
your son's violent behavior?
How do you plan to keep the
fact that he's a woman beater
a secret if he becomes a
public figure? It won't work
anymore.

                    CELARA
Now, don't you worry about
that, Tolly. I'll just make
one call to the police chief
and let him know that we won't
press charges.

                    TOLLY (frowning)
Press charges on who?

Celara smiles into the rear view mirror.

She smoothes back her hair forced by rigor mortis into a
sleek bun.

                    CELARA
The chief is our very good
friend, you see. He deals
quite well with threats
against me and my son.

                    TOLLY
I never threatened you,
Celara. Or Alex.

                    CELARA (sobbing)
          I happen to be in fear of my
          life from a woman who attacked
          a mayoral candidate in front
          of his wife and children and
          then kidnapped his mother, an
          elderly woman, to intimidate
          her into silence about what
          she witnessed.

                    TOLLY
          That's a lie!

                    CELARA
          Not by the time I'm done
          talking. Likely, the chief
          will even find my credit cards
          in   your   apartment   with
          unauthorized charges on them.
          Like for a new camera, say. To
          replace the camera you broke
          when you attacked my son. Who
          do you think they'll believe?

Tolly looks stunned.

                    TOLLY
          My camera's not broken.

                    CELARA
          Seriously. Just throw your
          wildest guess out there. Who
          will they believe, Tolly? Hmm?
          Who?

                    TOLLY
          You can't do that.

                    CELARA
          One call and it's already
          done. One call from me and
          it's always done.

Tolly sinks back in the front seat.

                    CELARA
          You really should do the right
          thing, you know. You should do
          the right thing, right now.

Celara glances at the shoulder bag that Tolly clutches to
her chest as a shield.

                    CELARA
          Don't   make   a   mistake   that
          haunts you   for   the   rest   of
          your life.

                    TOLLY
          Open this door.

                    CELARA
          For instance, now would be a
          great time for the right thing
          to happen.

Tolly sighs and lets her shoulders slump and her head
droop.

                    TOLLY
          I've   seen   just   about
          everything in this city. But
          never in my entire life...
          did   I   ever   think   it
          possible... for a barracuda
          to give birth to a shark.

Celara's eyes widen with shock while that sinks in.

                    CELARA (enraged)
          You uppity Black bitch! Who
          do you think you are? You're
          nothing! Nothing!

Celara reaches for her glove box.

Tolly whips the camera tripod out of her bag with one hand
and uses it to block the glove box.

> TOLLY
> I'm the one holding the
> camera.

> CELARA
> Have you lost your mind? One
> call. Remember?

> TOLLY
> Have you lost the primary?

Tolly turns the camera in her other hand so that Celara
can see the record light.

> TOLLY
> Like I said. Not broken.

Celara's eys narrow.

> CELARA
> You can't use that. You
> recorded me without my
> permission.

> TOLLY
> It can't be used in a court of
> law, no. But an amazing type
> of justice happens in the
> court of public opinion. Just
> your wildest guess, Celara.
> Who do you think they'll
> believe?

Celara doesn't answer.

> TOLLY
> You know that I'm right. You
> know how this works.

Celara holds up a cell phone.

                    CELARA
          I know exactly how this works.
          One call. If not to the chief
          of police then someone much
          worse who *will not like you*.

                    TOLLY
          Can you dial faster than I can
          upload this video?

Tolly holds up the camera.

Long pause.

Celara releases the child lock.

                    CELARA
          Get out of my car.

Tolly stands on the sidewalk in front of her three-flat.

Celara's car glides away into traffic.

Tolly makes a call on her cell phone.

                    TOLLY
          Tina. It went like we thought
          it might. By the way, when
          Grendel's mother showed up,
          and it went to a completely
          different level. (pause) No.
          I'm okay. But send someone to
          my building, just in case.

Tolly attaches her camera to to phone.

                    TOLLY
          By the way, have you ever seen
          a barracuda give birth to a
          shark? Well brace yourself.

FADE OUT
THE END

Screenplay 8

Faraway, Iowa

CAST OF CHARACTERS

The Woman - Black female, mid 30s to mid 40s

The Man - mid 30s to mid 40s

TIME
Near future.

FADE IN

EXT. IOWA - MIDDAY

Sunshine.

Clear skies.

Cornfields.

Corn silos.

Windmills.

Barns.

Haystacks.

Two-story, weathered, prairie-style house.

Domestic drones patrol a lonely road.

INT. IOWA:HOUSE:BATHROOM - LATE AFTERNOON

A WOMAN in silhouette shades her eyes to gaze at the
sunset through a window.

But she's not really shielding her eyes.

She's holding the results of a pregnancy test and crying.

She vomits into the toilet.

INT. IOWA:HOUSE:KITCHEN - DUSK

There is a shopping list on the refrigerator door.

The woman smiles over her shoulder and grabs the list.

She picks up a recyclable shopping bag.

210   Lee McQueen

She waves to a MAN sitting on the couch playing an interactive game that takes up an entire wall of the home.

Involved with the game, he doesn't wave back.

EXT. IOWA:TRUCK:ROAD - DUSK

A drone follows the woman's truck.

INT/EXT. IOWA:TRUCK:GROCERY STORE:PARKING LOT - NIGHT

The woman sits in the driver's seat in a lot three-quarters full.

The drone circles above the truck.

Someone is next to the woman in the passenger seat.

A scarecrow.

The woman removes her cell phone and other electronics, and tucks them into the pocket of the scarecrow's overalls.

She picks up the recyclable grocery bag, locks the truck doors, and walks into the grocery store's front entrance.

The drone circles above the truck.

INT. IOWA:GROCERY STORE - NIGHT

The woman walks down an empty store aisle, and then out the back door.

EXT. IOWA:EMPTY FIELDS - NIGHT

The woman runs.

EXT. IOWA:BARN - NIGHT

The woman approaches a creepy barn.

Rusted hulks of ancient farm equipment create shadows.

INT. IOWA:BARN - NIGHT

The woman counts money and lays it on a long table with stirrups.

A hand scoops the money away and covers the table with a big white sheet of paper.

The hand hovers over a tray of sharp instruments

The woman stares at the barn's ceiling, unshed tears filling her eyes.

Time passes.

The woman opens her eyes.

She sits up to find herself alone.

A cocktail of pills sits in a cup next to a glass of water.

The woman swallows the pills.

EXT. IOWA:BARN - NIGHT

The woman walks out of the barn.

A drone circles overhead, but she doesn't notice.

INT. IOWA:GROCERY STORE - NIGHT

The woman pays for groceries.

INT. IOWA:HOUSE:KITCHEN - NIGHT

The husband puts away the groceries and cooks.

INT. IOWA:HOUSE:BATHROOM - NIGHT

The woman cries.

EXT. IOWA:HOUSE - NIGHT

Moon and stars illuminate...

Cornfields that whisper secrets.

Tall corn silos that loom and cast huge shadows.

Windmills that slice the air.

Barn doors that creak open.

Haystacks that crunch under stealthy footsteps.

The shadow of several drones that cross over the two-story, weathered, prairie-style house.

A fleet of law enforcement cars that drive down the road and surround the house.

FADE OUT
THE END

Screenplay 9

Deep in the Woods

CAST OF CHARACTERS

The Woman - Black, female, mid 40s

The Man - mid 40s

TIME
Near future.

FADE IN

INT. - STONE CABIN - NIGHT

A baseball bat is propped next to the front door.

A lit candle sits on a table.

A handwritten note demands:

"Give us the women or we kill everyone."

A sad-eyed WOMAN sits in a chair across from an angry MAN.

                    WOMAN
          Do they want your mother too?

                    MAN (snarling)
          What the hell do you think?
          She's seventy-five for God's
          sake.

                    WOMAN (sarcastic)
          So just your wife and
          daughter. That's it?

                    MAN
          Or they'll kill all of us.

                    WOMAN
          We can't do it. I don't care
          about my life as much as hers.
          She's too young to have to
          face this.

                    MAN
          So's our son.

                    WOMAN
          She hasn't lived. She's our
          baby.

                    MAN
So's our son. He's lived less
than everyone here.

                    WOMAN
I know. But it's wrong. You
know what they'll do to her.
I'll do it, but not her. I'll
go so she doesn't...

                    MAN
They want you both.

                    WOMAN
There has to be another way.

                    MAN
We've been through every
option at least three times
the last forty days! They'll
starve us out. Burn us out.
Or shoot us out. We're
surrounded and outgunned.

                    WOMAN
Maybe we could just reason
with them...

                    MAN
Reason with people wearing
the skins of other people?
Rapists and cannibals? What
do you plan to say? Those
people out there are no
longer human. It would be
easier to reason with one of
the feral dogs scavenging the
city.

                    WOMAN
But...

                    MAN
          But nothing! There's no one
          to help us. Everybody's dead
          or they turned into those
          predators (pointing outside)
          who drink blood like water.
          Anything to survive. No one's
          riding to the rescue. No
          police. No national guard. No
          military. Nothing. NOTHING!

                    WOMAN
          Then what?

The man looks away.

                    WOMAN
          What?

The man shakes his head.

                    MAN
          You know what has to happen.

                    WOMAN
          It doesn't have to. We are
          still a family. Not beasts
          like them.

                    MAN
          Are you sure about that? After
          civilization went back to the
          Stone Age, we all became
          beasts.

                    WOMAN
          We're not like them.

                    MAN
          No. We don't hang human
          skeletons from our fence. Yet.
          But who knows what we'll do in
          a few months just to stay
          alive. Maybe even weeks. Days.

                    WOMAN
          Tonight?

                    MAN
          WE'RE OUT OF RESOURCES!

The woman sighs.

                    MAN
          We don't have any food. We
          have two days' worth of water.
          After that, we're dead anyway
          and it won't matter.

The woman shakes her head.

                    MAN
          They've been out there for
          forty days. They won't leave
          until they get what they came
          for. (pause) At least this
          way...

                    WOMAN
          What do you mean "at least
          this way?"

                    MAN
          I can't fight them all. I
          can't protect you or her.

                    WOMAN
          No. Obviously, you can't.

The man stares at the woman for a long moment.

                    MAN
They're stronger. And there's
more of them.

                    WOMAN
Don't say it. I can't bear to
hear that filth come out of
your mouth.

                    MAN
With them, you and she might
live. You have... a chance.

                    WOMAN
To become like them? To be
their pets? Slaves? How do you
even know we'll live? Maybe
our skeletons will hang off
the hoods of their trucks and
their motorcycles too.

                    MAN
They want women. They want...

The woman makes a gagging sound.

                    MAN
They want... to breed. That
means...

                    WOMAN (whispering)
Please stop. Stop talking.

                    MAN
We're out of options. There's
no   more   ammunition.   My
mother's barely alive as it
is. Our son's too young to
fight and he's starving to
death.

                    WOMAN
          So you'll trade us? Me and
          her? So you can live?

Long silence.

EXT. - STONE HOUSE - NIGHT

Shadowy silhouettes surround the house.

Bonfires create more shadows.

Chanting.

Drums beat louder.

INT. STONE HOUSE - NIGHT

                    WOMAN
          I thought I understood this
          world. I thought I understood
          you. But I didn't understand
          a single thing.

                    MAN
          Would you rather we all died?

The woman sobs.

                    MAN
          Since you can't decide, maybe
          we should ask her what *she*
          would do to save her younger
          brother's life.

                    WOMAN
          And yours?

Long silence.

                    WOMAN (disgusted)
          Even feral dogs care for their
          young.

Too angry to speak, the man stands.

He turns his back and walks away to a peep hole.

He looks outside.

The silhouettes still surround the house.

The drums beat louder.

EXT. STONE HOUSE - NIGHT

The people surrounding the house chant even louder.

INT. STONE HOUSE - NIGHT

                    MAN (quietly)
          She's dying anyway.

                    WOMAN
          But we don't have to kill her.

                    MAN
          Or you?

Silence.

The woman shakes her head.

                    WOMAN
          Don't you do that. You are in
          no position to judge me.

                    MAN
We can't get any more
antivirals with those
monsters out there. How much
longer do you think she'll
last?

                    WOMAN
Just because she had a
boyfriend who... (shaking her
head) You've become a cruel
man. Or maybe you always
were.

                    MAN (shouting)
And maybe you can't face the
reality of a cruel world!
She's getting sicker! If we
send her out there...

                    WOMAN
If *you* send US out there.
Like you said...

                    MAN
Like *they* said.

                    WOMAN
They want us both.

The man paces.

                    MAN
If they acquire the virus and
pass it around among
themselves, then they die
too.

The woman cries again.

                    WOMAN
They'll pass *her* around. And
me too.

                    MAN
          It's the ONLY WAY!

                    WOMAN
          God help us. Please. If You
          even exist anymore, please
          help us.

Running feet.

A door slams.

The woman and man run to the front door which is wide
open.

The woman screams.

                    WOMAN
          She's gone! Oh my God. She
          heard you. She ran out there!
          To them!

The man stands in the doorway, undecided.

                    WOMAN (shrieking)
          Do something!

The man doesn't move.

The chanting stops.

A roar goes up from the darkness.

The woman runs out of the front door wailing.

                    WOMAN
          Noooo! Don't hurt her!

The man lifts his arm to stop her. Then he drops his arm
to his side.

He bows his head.

More roars from the crowd.

When the screaming of his wife and daughter starts, the man closes the front door, locks it, and sinks to the floor sobbing.

He grabs the baseball bat by the door and starts wrecking the room.

EXT. STONE HOUSE - DAWN

Engines roar in the distance.
Burnt out fires, bloody clothing, pieces of flesh, and trash surround the steel gate.

Bones hang from the steel gate.

INT. STONE HOUSE - DAWN

The table and a chair is broken.

The candle is smashed on the floor.

The bloody baseball bat lays on the floor in the center of the room.

Beside the baseball bat the other chair lays on its side.

Above the chair, the man swings from a noose.

FADE OUT
THE END

Screenplay 10

Johnnie Ganjaweed

CAST OF CHARACTERS

Paris - Black, female, early 20s

Ole Girl - Black, female, 70s

Tattoo Artist - early 20s

Rancher - White, mid-40s

Coworker (voice only)

Probation Officer (voice only)

Drug Dealer (voice only)

Police Officer (voice only)

News Reader (voice only)

Elderly Woman #1 (voice only)

Middle-aged Man #1 (voice only)

Elderly Woman #2 (voice only)

Elderly Man #1 (voice only)

Young Man #1 (voice only)

Middle-aged Woman (voice only)

Young Woman (voice only)

Middle-aged Man #2 (voice only)

Middle-aged Man #3 (voice only)

Young Man #2 (voice only)

TIME
Near future.

FADE IN

EXT. PRISON:ALABAMA - DAY

PARIS finds OLE GIRL on the yard with a group of other older women who play cards.

Paris waits for Ole Girl to win.

Paris and Ole Girl walk off a ways.

Paris hands Ole Girl a baggy full of pills.

There is a visible scar on Paris's shoulder.

Ole Girl folds bills into a book and passes it to Paris.

> PARIS
> Who are our heroes now, G?

> OLE GIRL
> Who indeed?

> PARIS
> Took me three weeks, but I got through those books. I even went back to the encyclopedias. I can't believe you gave me homework.

> OLE GIRL
> Good reading, hunh?

> PARIS
> That Underground Railroad was alright. We need one around here.

Paris looks around at concrete and steel surrounding the yard.

                    PARIS
Nat Turner and Harriet Tubman?
Now that's straight gangster.
Ride   or   die   for   real.
Frederick Douglass too.

                    OLE GIRL
They don't make 'em like they
used to.

                    PARIS
They sure don't. Revolution.
Freedom.

                    OLE GIRL
What happened to the John
Browns? The Denmark Veseys?

                    PARIS
If you don't know, I sure
don't.

                    OLE GIRL
Now W.E.B. DuBois was for
education and Booker T.
Washington for economics
during Jim Crow. They stood up
in a different sort of way.
Ida B. Wells against lynching.
Martin Luther King Jr for
desegregation.

Paris nods.

                    OLE GIRL
Paris, it took one hundred
years after slavery *supposedly*
ended for Malcolm X and Huey
Newton and Angela Davis to
rise up. Who has that kind of
time? Life is short!

Paris stares into the middle distance.

                    OLE GIRL
          Nobody   gives   power   away,
          girl. All   that   'work   within
          the   system'   is   a   dream.
          That's   lying   to   yourself.
          Some   laws   just   have   to   be
          broken.

Paris narrows her eyes at the familiar phrase.

                    OLE GIRL (shaking head)
          Nope. Nobody is gonna just lay
          down and say, 'take my power
          so   you   can   have   some   for
          yourself.'   Nope.   The   world
          never worked that way. Never.

Paris searches Ole Girl's eyes then slowly pulls a piece
of paper from her waistband.

Ole Girl checks their surroundings then nods.

                    PARIS
          Neither   slavery   nor
          involuntary servitude, except
          as   a   punishment   for   crime
          whereof the party shall have
          been   dully   convicted,   shall
          exist   within   the   United
          States, or any place subject
          to their jurisdiction.

                    OLE GIRL
          Except.   That's   some
          exception, isn't it Paris?
          Like I said, it never went
          away.

Paris nods.

                    PARIS
          Look G. You sure about your
          new hookup?

                    OLE GIRL
          Nobody's gonna mess with an
          old geezer like me. What for?

Paris shrugs.

                    OLE GIRL
          I know somebody. Won't beat
          your customer service, but
          that's alright. Frankly, I
          prefer my own batch that I
          used to mix up in the ole
          chemistry lab.

                    PARIS
          You were the best chemistry
          teacher I ever had, G. You
          know I never cheated in your
          class.

                    OLE GIRL
          Warms my heart. But it broke
          my heart when you had to leave
          school. Didn't like that at
          all.

                    OLE GIRL
          Don't come back here, Paris.
          After you leave, I don't want
          to ever see you again.

Old Girl hugs Paris.

There is a visible scar on Old Girl's shoulder too.

Paris hides tears, then nods.

                    OLE GIRL
          If you look hard enough,
          you'll find the hero.

EXT. PRISON:ALABAMA - DAY

Paris stands alone as steel gates slowly open, rubbing her
left shoulder.

Lonely blacktop road leads to nothingness.

EXT. PROBATION OFFICE:ALABAMA - DAY

Paris hesitates, then walks in.

INT. PROBATION OFFICE:ALABAMA - DAY

A scanner by the door catches the implant in Paris's
shoulder.

Her file appears on a large screen.

A long silence greets her.

Paris moves towards a chair.

> PROBATION OFFICER (voice)
> You're in *my* house now, girl.
> Did I say you could sit on *my*
> chair?

Time passes while Paris stands. Finally...

> PROBATION OFFICER (voice)
> ...no contact with family
> members, past associates and
> acquaintances. No alcohol or
> drugs... No weapons...
> Immediate employment from the
> list of approved employers...
> weekly drug tests—hair and
> urine samples... You may not
> leave city limits...

The probation officer drones on.

Paris checks her file on the large screen.

Her charge is possession of marijuana with intention to distribute.

> PROBATION OFFICER (voice)
> Hard to believe anyone with sense would throw away a college education for prison, but damn if that's not exactly what you did.

> PARIS
> It was to pay for tuition and books. That's all.

> PROBATION OFFICER (voice)
> That's all it ever is. Mommy and Daddy couldn't afford the med school tab?

Paris flinches.

> PROBATION OFFICER (voice)
> Oh yeah. Definitely issues there. Well, you should have sold ass just like everyone else. Then you wouldn't have gotten jammed up. At least not too hard. (chuckling) The warden says you come highly recommended. Maybe we can work out a nice little trade arrangement for you.

The Probation Officer looks Paris up and down and compares what he sees to Paris's revealing scan on the large screen and grins.

Paris looks at him without expression.

A long silence passes.

> PROBATION OFFICER (voice)
> Okaaay. Not interested in the
> house special. Latrine duty,
> kitchen duty, yard duty.
> That's what's on the menu for
> today. What'll it be?

EXT. URBAN FARM:ALABAMA - DAY

Paris tends to a row of vegetables in the hot sun.

Tired and sweaty, she rubs the scar on her shoulder again.

INT. APARTMENT: ALABAMA - NIGHT

Paris replays a phone message from her mother.

> MOTHER (voice)
> Paris, I know that you've been
> calling here and hanging up.
> Listen to me carefully. Please
> do not call again, because
> your father's already
> wondering who's at this
> number. I covered for you, but
> I can't keep doing that.

A tear forms in Paris's eye.

She pulls out a kid's book marked "DISCARDED." Titled,
"Johnny Appleseed."

EXT. MANSION: ALABAMA - DAY

Paris is doing landscape work with a crew of ex-offenders.

A COWORKER has a scar on her shoulder.

                    COWORKER (voice)
          They say she died from her
          diabetes complications.

                    PARIS
          Shit! Ole Girl was my friend.
          She was my teacher. We used to
          talk about all kinds of stuff.

                    COWORKER (voice)
          People say that the guards
          tossed her cell.

Paris narrows her eyes and picks up a bag of grass seed.

                    COWORKER (voice)
          Took contraband. Wouldn't give
          her medication back even when
          she begged for it.

Paris wheels around dropping the bag of grass seed,
enraged.

                    COWORKER (voice)
          That's what I heard anyway.

                    PARIS (pissed)
          They killed Ole Girl. For
          what? Who would want to do her
          dirty?

                    COWORKER (voice)
          Isn't that what they do?
          That's their job. To kill us
          and destroy us. We work. We
          pay taxes, but we can't vote.
          Can't attend school. Can't
          leave the city limits. Can't
          do nothing. What's the fucking
          point?

Paris picks up the bag again and and doesn't answer.

She scatters grass seed across a small section of huge
lawn.

INT. APARTMENT:ALABAMA - NIGHT

Paris holds the book on Johnny Appleseed while she listens
to another phone message.

> MOTHER (voice)
> Your sister's grown up and
> going to school now. I can't
> tell you where, but she's
> fine. Don't contact her
> either, Paris. You know what
> will happen if you do. I mean
> it. We don't want her to end
> up like... Anyway... this is
> my last call. If her father
> finds out, he'll report you to
> your p.o. Don't call our house
> ever again, Paris.

Paris shakes her head. Her eyes fill with tears.

She stares at the wall, hopeless.

INT. VAN:ALABAMA - NIGHT

> DRUG DEALER (voice)
> So imma do you just this
> one, little girl?

> PARIS
> Just this one.

> DRUG DEALER (voice)
> Yeah, well, get to know me.

The dealer grins and pushes a button on his cell phone,
starts whispering.

Paris exits the van.

>   DRUG DEALER (voice)
>   Get to know me, baby girl.
>   Listen, if you're ever short
>   on money, we can work out any
>   deal you want.

EXT. VACANT LOT:ALABAMA - NIGHT

Paris walks a few steps, then pauses to smell the weed.

The van's engine starts.

A truck with no headlights races alongside the van and slows.

Paris shrinks into the shadows.

Volt guns puncture the van's exterior.

The truck races away.

The smoking van tips over the embankment into a shallow creek.

Paris hesitates, then shoves the dimebag into her pants pocket, and runs down the embankment.

The truck is upside down, crumpled, and riddled with scorch marks.

The drug dealer sprawls halfway out of the window crushed around his torso, neck broken.

>   PARIS
>   Motherfuck.

Paris swallows.

She hears a screech of car tires from above.

Voices shout in the dark.

She enters the van through a window.

INT. VAN:ALABAMA - NIGHT

Volt guns and cash are scattered around a bag.

Paris ignores the guns, snatches the cash, and shoves the
cash into the bag.

EXT. VAN:ALABAMA - NIGHT

Backing out of the window, Paris sees dark silhouettes
against the the night sky.

The silhouettes point her direction.

Paris runs.

INT: TATTOO PARLOR:ALABAMA - NIGHT

                    TATTOO ARTIST
          Cash or trade?

                    PARIS
          Cash.

                    TATTOO ARTIST
          Well, fuck. For cash, I guess
          I'll sterilize my equipment.

Paris winces.

                    TATTOO ARTIST
          C'mon. I'm kidding. I went to
          med school and everything.

                    PARIS (dubious)
          Med school.

                    TATTOO ARTIST
          I went to the med school to
          catch my bus this morning.

                    PARIS
          Now look.

                    TATTOO ARTIST
          I'm just winding you up. I get
          bored here by myself. I know
          what I'm doing. Let's go.

The tattoo artist zaps all of Paris's prison tattoos with
a hand held laser.

He paints the burn marks with a small brush.

                    TATTOO ARTIST
          Done. Marks go away in two
          days.

He hands Paris a lollipop.

                    TATTOO ARTIST
          That's for not crying. Hate
          that shit. Two thousand.

Paris looks in the bag to get the money. She frowns,
puzzled by something.
She hands over the money, then she grabs her shirt.

The tattoo artist sterilizes instruments and equipment.

                    TATTOO ARTIST (casually)
          Sometimes we get people in
          here   that   had   a
          misunderstanding with Uncle
          Sam. Acquired a little bit of
          circuit   work   they   don't
          really need. We recycle it.

A long pause. Paris looks at her shoulder.

                    PARIS
          My circuit work needs a heart
          beat.   The   minute   that
          heartbeat stops, they come for
          my dead body and check me off
          the list of things to do.

                    TATTOO ARTIST
          Yeah. That's lousy. But look,
          you know what… some laws were
          made to be broken. Don't you
          think?

Paris blinks.

                    PARIS
          Right. Some laws need to be
          broken.

                    TATTOO ARTIST
          Five thousand. Price includes
          liquid bone injections.

                    PARIS
          Liquid fucking what?

                    TATTOO ARTIST
          For   your   face   and   teeth.
          Defeats facial recognition. It
          only takes a little. Up to
          you.

                    PARIS
          Do it.

                    TATTOO ARTIST
          I'll tell you right now, it
          hurts like a mother. I can't
          put you under. You might not
          wake up.

                    PARIS (sighing)
          Rock me, Amadeus.

The Tattoo Artist opens a drawer that holds scalpels, long needles, scissors, and other surgical equipment.

Paris's eyes go wide.

> PARIS (swallowing)
> Remember, I'm paying cash.

> TATTOO ARTIST
> Relax, your ass. I run a
> clean house. Hang on.

The Tattoo Artist disappears out the back door.

> PARIS
> Where the hell are you going?

The Tattoo Artist re-enters with a puppy.

> TATTOO ARTIST
> His heart beats just fine.

Twenty minutes later, five thousand dollars lay on a side table.

Paris and the Tattoo Artist smoke weed. Paris loads up on pain pills.

> TATTOO ARTIST
> Told you it would hurt.

> PARIS
> Yeah. You told me.

The puppy sleeps in a dog bed in a corner of the room with a bandage between its neck and shoulder.

> PARIS
> What'll happen to the dog? You
> don't hurt him, do you?

                    TATTOO ARTIST (indignant)
          The hell you take me for? I
          don't fucking kill dogs.
          That's sick.

                    PARIS
          Fuck *me*. I just asked.

                    TATTOO ARTIST
          We drop him to the city pound
          once he heals. Buys you two
          weeks go time.

Paris tips the Tattoo Artist fifty dollars.

Startled, the Tattoo Artist disappears the money with
quick hands.

                    TATTOO ARTIST
          Look, I got some extra gear
          in the back. You look like
          you got places to go. Things
          to do. Whatever. Help
          yourself.

Paris grips the Tattoo Artists's hand.

                    TATTOO ARTIST
          By the way, stay of the grid.
          Disappear, girl. And don't
          come back. I don't do repeat
          visits. I see you again, I
          shake your hand with this.

The Tattoo Artist picks up a volt gun.

                    TATTOO ARTIST
          Get it?

Paris nods.

                    PARIS
          Got it.

                    TATTOO ARTIST
          I mean it. There's the road.
          Hit it.

EXT. TATTOO PARLOR:LOUISIANA - NIGHT

Paris looks into the money bag, feels around carefully.

                    PARIS (whispering)
          Some laws need to be broken.

EXT. ROAD:ALABAMA - NIGHT

Paris slouches behind the tree line of an old abandoned
highway.

INT. THRIFT STORE:ALABAMA - DAY

Paris sees stacks of tiny Mormon Bibles and Jehovah's
Witnesses booklets.

She dumps the booklets on the counter.

Then she throws an old road atlas on top of the booklets.

Then she wheels an old bicycle out the door.

EXT. RURAL ROAD:ALABAMA - DAY

The wind blows through Paris's hair while she rides the
bike.

A police officer stops Paris.

                    POLICE OFFICER
          Ma'am, do you need help?

                    PARIS (enthusiastically)
          I'm a witness for the Lord.
          He's all the help I need.

                    POLICE OFFICER (voice)
               As am I. What do have in that
               bag there?

The police officer scans Paris's shoulder, face, and
teeth.

                    PARIS
               Sir, in this bag, I have
               information that will change
               your life! Did you know that
               Jesus Christ died...

                    POLICE OFFICER (voice)
               Thank you, that will be all,
               ma'am.

                    PARIS
               But I was just about to...

                    POLICE OFFICER (voice)
               Thank you for your cooperation
               with law enforcement ma'am.
               Please proceed on your way and
               have a nice day.

Paris rides away on her creaky, old bike.

EXT. RURAL ROAD:LOUISIANA - DAY

Paris rides her bike along rural highways and byways and
back roads.

She waves at no one along road sides, farms, parks,
streams, creeks, riverbeds, bayous, swamps, and backyards.

She makes marks on the road atlas.

She visits the well-to-do who gives her glasses of water
and allows her to pick fruit from their trees.

She waves a happy hello and good-bye to everyone.

EXT. CHURCH:LOUISIANA - NIGHT

Paris sleeps on a church's patio furniture.

She waves goodbye to the church.

EXT. RURAL ROAD:TEXAS - DAY

A speeding pickup truck runs Paris off the road.

The truck driver hits the brakes and backs up.

Paris rights herself in the ditch, stuffing marijuana seeds back into the back pack.

A woman in a Rancher hat and boots stares down.

Paris experiences a moment of icy déjà vu remembering how the drug dealer's killers looked down the embankment at her.

Paris sees a gun in the Rancher's truck rack.

Paris holds the bicycle in front of herself as a shield.

> RANCHER
> You know it's fixin' to rain,
> doncha, hon? Look up at the
> sky.

Paris looks up.

> RANCHER
> It's gonna lightning and
> thunder real bad.

> PARIS
> Yeah, I'm gonna try to find
> some place to wait it out.

> RANCHER
> I'm just up the road.

Paris just looks at her.

                RANCHER
          Least I can do for running you
          off the road. How about it?

Paris pushes the bike out of the ditch.

The Rancher helps Paris put the bike in the truck bed.
Paris keeps the back pack with her in the truck's cab.

INT. RANCHER'S HOUSE:KITCHEN:TEXAS - DAY

Paris eats a huge bowl of chili and rice.

                PARIS
          My parents said I could use
          the summer to speak of God's
          glory to the world before I
          start med school this fall.
          Said it would teach me
          maturity and understanding
          and that I would be blessed
          in the... uh kingdom of
          heaven.

She hands the Rancher one of the little Bibles.

                RANCHER
          You know they have these on
          the Internet. You don't have
          to carry all these books in
          the heat and ride a bicycle
          all by yourself.

                PARIS
          But the books don't require
          an Internet connection.
          Somethings have to be done
          in-person. I always ask
          myself, What would Jesus do?

                    RANCHER
          Um hm. You got a answer for
          everything, seems like.

                    PARIS (carefully)
          No, but... God does.

The rancher eyes Paris with suspicion at the little Bible
and harrumphs a bit.

                    RANCHER
          You can use the shower if you
          need to and wash some clothes.

INT. RANCHER'S HOUSE:KITCHEN:TEXAS - DAY

Paris sleeps on the using the bag of booklets as a pillow.

EXT. RANCHER'S HOUSE:TEXAS - DAY

Paris waves good-bye.

EXT. COUNTRYSIDE:TEXAS - DAY

Paris explores shacks, barns, underneath rail bridges, and
ditches.

Waves at the countryside.

EXT. COUNTRYSIDE:TEXAS - NIGHT

Paris climbs into an abandoned rail car.

EXT. SMALL TOWN:GAS STATION:TEXAS - DAY

Paris washes up in the bathroom.

EXT. SMALL TOWN:LIBRARY:TEXAS - DAY

Paris makes copies of maps.

Paris wakes up on church steps, patio furniture, and inside gazebos.

EXT. SMALL TOWN:TEXAS - DAY

Paris waves at people on porches.

She talks to more police officers and passes out booklets to them.

EXT. COUNTRYSIDE:TEXAS - DAY

Paris picks fruit from trees and berries from bushes.

Waves good-bye to the brush.

EXT. ROAD:TEXAS - DAY

Paris hitches a ride in the back of a pick-up truck across scrubby, rocky West Texas.

EXT. ROAD:NEW MEXICO & ARIZONA - DAY

Paris hitches another ride in a hippie school bus across New Mexico and Arizona.

EXT. ROAD:CALIFORNIA - DAY

In southern California, Paris waves at ditches and farms on the route into Los Angeles.

In Los Angeles, Paris waves at vacant lots, parks, botanical gardens, front yards, backyards, and decorative greenery surrounding tech centers.

Paris smiles with pure joy.

EXT. ROAD:CALIFORNIA - DAY

Paris hitches another ride across Western desert.

EXT. ROAD:ARIZONA & NEW MEXICO - DAY

Paris pushes her bike up mountains, then coasts down.

She waves at hikers, bikers, vacationers, and vagrants.

EXT. ROAD:OKLAHOMA - DAY

Paris bikes across the plains waving through rain and
wind.

EXT. RANCHER:FRONT PORCH:TEXAS - DAY

Paris stops at the Rancher's driveway for old times sake.

The Rancher pulls in from the road with a grim look.

The Rancher opens the truck door, gets her shotgun from
the rack, and slams the door shut.

The Rancher places the shotgun on the open gate of the
pickup truck and folds her arms.

                    RANCHER
          Little   girl,   I   may   look
          redneck, but I know a thing or
          two. Or three.

Paris eyes the shotgun and begins to back away.

The Rancher puts her hand on the shotgun.

                    RANCHER
          You do not want to do that.

Paris waits.

                    RANCHER
          People go by how you look. You
          look a certain way, tell them
          a little something, then they
          fill in the rest for you.

The Rancher tightens grip on the shotgun.

                    RANCHER
          But you know all about that,
          don't you?

Paris looks concerned.

                    RANCHER
          I'm supposed to believe you're
          a Jehovah's Witness *and* a
          Mormon? You and this little
          holy roller routine, fooling
          folk with foolish talk.
          (snorts) But not me.

                    PARIS
          Nope. Not you.

                    RANCHER
          Nope. *Not* me. Specially after
          I saw what pushed up in my
          ditch and my backyard a month
          after you left. You're one of
          them ganjaweeds, aren't you?

                    PARIS (confused)
          Ganja whos?

The Rancher picks up the shotgun.

                    RANCHER
          Guess I got to show you,
          don't I? Shall we take a
          look?

                    PARIS
              After you.

                    RANCHER
              No. *You* first.

EXT. RANCHER'S HOUSE:BACKYARD:TEXAS - DAY

The Rancher marches Paris to a section behind the barn
piled with rusted metal.

The Rancher gestures with Paris to enter an opening in the
junk pile.

Inside the junk pile, is a waist-high patch of marijuana.

Paris notes that she is totally invisible from the road,
and tries to calculate an escape from the Rancher.

                    RANCHER
              Now, *look* you. I'm ex-
              military. I see the look in
              your eyes. Whatever you're
              thinking, I already thought.
              Let's not have a
              misunderstanding out here in
              the middle of nowhere where
              no one can hear you scream.
              Okay?

Paris looks at the volt gun with resignation.

                    RANCHER
              See here? You see all this?
              Look at this foolishness.

The Rancher points with the shotgun at the crowd of lush
and leafy weeds.

                    RANCHER
          Why would you do something
          like this and not even do it
          right? Why waste the time? My
          time. Your time. That's the
          part I don't understand.

Paris blinks.

                    RANCHER
          You young people need to
          think things all the way
          through. Listen to your
          elders sometime. You gotta
          learn to remove the male
          plants. Otherwise, it's no
          good. I'm telling you
          something for free, girl. You
          listening?

Paris stares in wonder.

                    RANCHER
          What are you, a slow-wit?

The Rancher, jabs the volt gun towards the plants.

                    PARIS
          Yes.

                    RANCHER
          Yes, you're slow-wit?

                    PARIS
          I mean no.

                    RANCHER
          You don't know? Your parents
          never had you tested?

                    PARIS
          I'm not slow. I'm just...
          taken by surprise.

                    RANCHER
          Some laws were made to be
          broken.

The Rancher slaps her thigh, and cackles.

                    PARIS (swallowing)
          Some laws were made to be
          broken.

Paris chuckles tightly at first and then with enthusiasm.

                    RANCHER (still cackling)
          Joke's on you. Even my
          friends who are the law know
          that. They won't bother you,
          Paris. Long as you speak your
          mind at the right time. You
          know what to do. So does
          everyone else by now who's
          not stupid.

INT. RANCHER'S HOUSE:KITCHEN:TEXAS - NIGHT

On television is the evening news.

The Rancher and Paris smoke weed.

The Rancher flips from channel to channel.

                    ELDERLY WOMAN #1 (voice)
          I mailed a marijuana evergreen
          wreath to my sister for
          Christmas. She said she loves
          it!

EXT. COUNTRYSIDE - DAY

Insertion shot of Paris throwing seeds while she waves.

INT. RANCHER'S HOUSE:KITCHEN:TEXAS - NIGHT

>   MIDDLE-AGED MAN #1 (voice)
>   If I just had a full bar
>   stocked with rum, whiskey,
>   vodka, tequila, and gin like
>   the Chief of Police does,
>   driving around in a drunken
>   stupor that would have been
>   okay. But noooo...

>   POLICE OFFICER (voice)
>   Once they got inside, they
>   allegedly found the suspect
>   holding three large plastic
>   bags of what appeared to be
>   marijuana and associated
>   paraphernalia...

>   NEWS READER (voice)
>   As you can see from this map,
>   the initial reports came from
>   the southern and southwestern
>   United States. However, large
>   patches have been reported
>   from all four corners of the
>   country.

EXT. COUNTRYSIDE - DAY

Handfuls of marijuana seed fly through the air.

INT. RANCHER'S HOUSE:KITCHEN:TEXAS - NIGHT

>   ELDERLY WOMAN #2 (voice)
>   Oh when my arthritis kicks up,
>   I mix a little of it with mint
>   for a nice iced tea on a hot
>   afternoon. Plenty of sugar.
>   Would you like a glass?

EXT. COUNTRYSIDE - DAY

Insertion shot of Paris dropping seeds into a planter by a front door with one hand while she holds Bible tracts with another.

INT. RANCHER'S HOUSE:KITCHEN:TEXAS - NIGHT

              POLICE OFFICER (voice)
     Moving into the backyard,
     police discovered 57 marijuana
     plants, yielding a total of 47
     pounds of pot, Delaney said.
     Drug paraphernalia and nearly
     $8,000 in cash was also found.

              ELDERLY MAN #1 (voice)
     I get migraines.

              YOUNG MAN #1 (voice)
     I have glaucoma.

EXT. COUNTRYSIDE - DAY

Paris whirls and twirls throwing fistfuls of seeds right and left.

INT. RANCHER'S HOUSE:KITCHEN:TEXAS - NIGHT

              NEWS READER (voice)
     Apparently, the idea catches
     on as word continues to spread
     about Ganjaweed, the man many
     people believe responsible for
     the initial...

EXT. COUNTRYSIDE - DAY

A crop duster releases a load of seed over vast fields.

EXT. CITY - NIGHT

More crop dusters release loads of seeds at night over the
city.

INT. RANCHER'S HOUSE:KITCHEN:TEXAS - NIGHT

                    MIDDLE-AGED WOMAN #1
                    (voice)
          Is my marijuana organic? I
          don't want to be a negative
          Nancy, but where's the
          quality control? Who's
          looking out for consumer
          safety? We deserve a product
          that is pure and clean. Okay?
          That's all I'm saying.

EXT. COUNTRYSIDE:ROAD - DAY

Vacationers throw marijuana seeds out their car windows,
pickup trucks, hippie school buses, BMWs, and SUVs.

INT. RANCHER'S HOUSE:KITCHEN:TEXAS - NIGHT

                    YOUNG WOMAN #1 (voice)
          It would also result in less
          people turning to alcohol,
          becoming alcoholics and less
          drunk driving accidents. I'll
          just bet the alcohol lobby
          can't stand that.

                    MIDDLE-AGED MAN #2 (voice)
          Doctors   say   they   can't
          operate. I mean, what do I
          care? I only have three months
          left anyway. Some laws need to
          be broken. So fuck it. Come
          and arrest me. I'll be the one
          sitting in my fucking chair,
          reading a fucking book, not
          bothering anybody, and feeling
          no pain for once in my fucking
          fucked up life. Go ahead and
          fucking quote me on that. I
          don't give a fuck.

                    MIDDLE-AGED MAN #3 (voice)
          I got laid off when they shut
          the plant down. Why are we
          outsourcing and shipping our
          good   manufacturing   and
          processing jobs overseas to
          Colombian cartels? We can
          supply our own demand. I say,
          keep it local.

                    MIDDLE-AGED WOMAN #2 (voice)
          I use it to keep my blood
          pressure down because I can't
          afford regular medicine. Thank
          you, Ganjaweed!

INT. BOTANICAL GARDENS - DAY

Visitors drop seeds into an exotic patches of flowers.

INT. RANCHER'S HOUSE:KITCHEN:TEXAS - NIGHT

>   NEWS READER (voice)
>   Ganjaweed disciples use all
>   manner of warehouse   and
>   transportation networks to
>   process and package. Police
>   are currently reviewing their
>   strategy for dealing with this
>   new phenomenon. When marijuana
>   grows like dandelions in every
>   backyard, including that of
>   the Governor of Alabama, how
>   do you enforce the drug laws?

EXT. ALABAMA GOVERNOR'S MANSION - NIGHT

Wearing the clothes from her visit to the tattoo parlor,
Paris stares at the large residence and smiles.

INT. RANCHER'S HOUSE:KITCHEN:TEXAS - NIGHT

>   YOUNG MAN #2 (voice)
>   I sleep bad some nights. It
>   helps me with my PTSD. God
>   bless Ganjaweed!

>   RANCHER
>   Jesus Christ. You're not a
>   ganjaweed.   You're   the
>   Ganjaweed. It was *you* who got
>   it all started.

>   PARIS
>   I guess so.

>   RANCHER
>   I take back everything I said.
>   That *is* a job well-done.

                    NEWS READER (voice)
          In a strange reversal, a
          public that has half of its
          earnings earmarked for law
          enforcement at local, state,
          and   federal   level,   the
          unspoken theory of that sane
          public seems to be that some
          laws are made to be broken...

                    PARIS
          Did he say sane public?

                    NEWS READER (voice)
          Next thing you know, everyone
          will   stop   paying   taxes   and
          then where we would be?

The News Reader, Rancher, and Paris laugh together.

FADE OUT
THE END

Screenplay 11

Sunday

CAST OF CHARACTERS

#1 - Corporate, Male, Black, mid-30s to early 40s

#2 - Supply & Production, Male, mid-30s to early 40s

#3 - Transport & Security, Male, mid-30s to early 40s

#4 - Finance & Administration, Female, mid-30s to early 40s

#5 - Science & Research, Female, mid-30s to early 40s

#6 - Engineering, Female, mid-30s to early 40s

TIME
Near future.

FADE IN

EXT. BUILDING - DAY

One-by-one, TWO WOMEN and TWO MEN in dark suits and
sunglasses, with earbuds and throat mikes enter a
faceless, glass-fronted corporate building using their key
cards.

INT. BUILDING:LOBBY - DAY

One-by-one, the four mysterious people use their key cards
to enter a clear, bulletproof security door.

INT. BUILDING:HALLWAY - DAY

One-by-one, the four walk down the hallway with purpose.

INT. BUILDING:BOARDROOM - DAY

One-by-one, the four sit at a long glass-topped table set
for six people with a pitcher of water, glasses, pen, and
paper.

In front of each person is a sign:

#2 - Supply & Production

#3 - Transport & Security

#4 - Finance & Administration

#5 - Science & Research

#2 fiddles with his sign, puzzled.

The head of the table is empty but has a sign: #1 -
Corporate.

All four people eye the foot of the table and the sign #6 - Engineering.

Four sets of eyes glance at each other. Shoulders shrug.

They remove their sunglasses, throat mikes, and earbuds.

After a long silence, a MAN and a WOMAN enter the boardroom.

The man goes to the head of the table. The sign identifies him as #1 CORPORATE.

The woman goes to the foot of the table, #6 - Engineering.

Supply, Transport, Finance, and Science size up Engineering.

>   CORPORATE
>   Whenever you're ready, we'll
>   begin.

Attention returns to the head of the table.

>   CORPORATE
>   Thank you for coming in today.
>   I'll need your reports on old
>   business.

Supply side-eyes Engineering.

>   SUPPLY
>   We have a visitor.

>   CORPORATE
>   We do.

A long silence.

>   TRANSPORT
>   Our trucks have been serviced
>   for the year and retro-fitted
>   with additional self-defense
>   mechanisms and...

                    FINANCE
We solved the problem of
missing cash flow from the
border area. It turns out, our
neighbors to the North and
South   respond   to   other
incentives so...

                    SCIENCE
A few simple tweaks updated
the old formula to keep the
side-effects at a minimum. We
still   have   to   cut   it   to
keep...

                    SUPPLY
We needed to recruit personnel
to   acquire   the   amount   of
supply   needed   to   meet
increased demand. Therefore,
I...

                    CORPORATE
As I thought. Good work.

Corporate stands.

                    CORPORATE
Guns,   drugs,   gambling,
business   intelligence,
politics,   the   rest--all
reliable   earners.   Take   one
look around this room and you
find not one of us ever missed
a trick.

Supply, Transport, Finance, and Science smile with pride.

                    CORPORATE
          But the world is changing. New
          technology, new communication,
          new   energy,   new   economies.
          It's classic Darwin. Adapt or
          die.

Supply, Transport, Finance, and Science eye each other,
then #6 Engineering.

                    CORPORATE
          We need to be bold. We need to
          stay ahead of the game. Create
          new   markets,   always.   But
          always we supply, transport,
          finance, and research those
          markets.   So   relax.   Don't
          worry. The games change, but
          the names stay the same.

Supply, Transport, Finance, and Science nod and relax.

                    CORPORATE
          Has anyone guessed what we're
          about to do?

Silence, then...

                    TRANSPORT
          Real estate.

                    CORPORATE
          Halfway there. Anyone else?

Silence.

                    FINANCE (frowning)
          Energy?

                    CORPORATE (smug)
          You're getting warmer. All of
          you have a piece to the puzzle
          based on the research I asked
          you to do. So I'll need your
          reports on new business. I'm
          sure you'll figure it out once
          we get going.

Corporate uses a remote control to dim the lights, close
window shades, and starts a projector.

Corporate sits.

                    CORPORATE
          Supply. Go.

Supply, Transport, Finance, and Science click through
slides.

The slides show:

Fire, coal, windmills, water turbines, steam engines, oil,
gas, and biofuel.

Maps of diminishing energy resources and their
distribution points.

Maps of emerging energy resources, including the sun.

The room fills with excited whispers.

Three hours pass.

No one notices Corporate leave the room and come back in
with a cart loaded with food.

                    SCIENCE
          The   Research   Department
          patented a dirt cheap method
          to   manufacture   and process
          silicon   for   photovoltaic
          cells. We just need to build
          up   the   infrastructure,   the
          industry, and the demand.

Science takes a seat.

Corporate stands.

                    CORPORATE
          That's amazing research.

Corporate uses the remote control to switch off the
projector, raise the lights, and open the window shades.

                    CORPORATE
          Lunch on the back table and
          then questions.

Everyone mills around the back table.

Corporate moderates the questions that Supply, Transport,
Finance, and Science have for each other.

Another hour passes.

The questions peter out.

                    CORPORATE
          To control access to the most
          powerful   renewable   energy
          resource ever created is to
          rule the world. (Pause). But
          can we do it?

There's no answer.

                    CORPORATE
          To   not   submit   to   bribery
          demands of government leaders
          and their police forces means
          what?

Corporate spreads his hands.

                    CORPORATE
          Absolute. Power.

A silent thrill travels through the boardroom.

                    CORPORATE
          We have to move fast.

Silence.

Corporate eyes Engineering.

                    CORPORATE
          Well?

Engineering nods.

                    CORPORATE
          Based   on   what   she's   heard
          from you today, The Engineer
          says   yes.   But   what   do   you
          say?

Supply, Transport, Finance, and Science nod their heads
one-by-one.

Corporate walks toward the boardroom door.

                    CORPORATE
          Use the room to work out the
          time table. We have to
          outsource   our   current
          operations and plan the new
          operations.   Play   your
          positions. The Engineer is
          your go to until the next
          meeting two days from now.
          I'll take your updates then.

Supply, Transport, Finance, Science, and Engineering watch
Corporate leave.

Supply, Transport, Finance, Science turn to Engineering
who seems prepared for the scrutiny.

                    SUPPLY
          So how did Corporate find you?

                    ENGINEERING
          I graduated top of my class
          from   one   of   the   most
          prestigious   engineering
          schools in the nation. Did
          field work in various energy
          plants   for   fifteen   years
          before   I   joined   my
          university's faculty. Came up
          for tenure. Plagiarism charge.
          No tenure. No warm welcome
          back to the field either.
          Corporate didn't seem to mind
          all that.

                    SUPPLY
          No. He never does.

Supply gives a jaunty wave.

                    SUPPLY
          Pharmacist   who   over-
          prescribed.

Transport grunts.

>   TRANSPORT
>   Military   transporter.
>   Dishonorable discharge.

>   FINANCE (smirking)
>   Banker. Money launderer on the
>   side.

Science laughs.

>   SCIENCE
>   Chemistry major. Recreational
>   demolitionist on the weekend.

Engineering grins.

>   ENGINEERING
>   Oh, the places we'll go. This
>   is gonna be fun.

>   SUPPLY
>   So whose idea was it to take
>   over the world? Yours or
>   Corporate's?

>   ENGINEERING
>   Corporate's running this show.
>   He found me because he needed
>   someone who could build. He's
>   the ringmaster. I'm the
>   circus.

Supply, Transport, Finance, and Science laugh.

>   SCIENCE
>   Aren't we all?

>   TRANSPORT
>   Get started on the timeline.
>   You know Corporate's strict on
>   deadlines.

INT. OFFICE - DAY

Supply, Transport, Finance, Science, and Engineering argue with each other in the middle of charts, graphs, spreadsheets, computer screens, maps, and illustrations.

Corporate comes in to yell at them.

Supply, Transport, Finance, Science shake their heads and yell back at Corporate.

Corporate ticks discussion points off on his fingers. Then waits for a response, arms akimbo.

Supply, Transport, Finance, Science, and Engineering stare in defiance, then nod reluctant agreement.

Corporate leaves the room.

INT. WAREHOUSE - DAY

                    CORPORATE
          Did you get it arranged?

                    ENGINEERING
          We need at least another
          month.

                    CORPORATE (shouting)
          You have *exactly* two weeks!

Engineering shakes her head, exasperated.

Corporate responds to that with a steely stare.

Engineering throws up her hands in surrender.

                    ENGINEERING
          Okay!

Corporate leaves the warehouse.

Engineering gives Finance a significant look.

                    ENGINEERING
          You heard him.

Corporate lingers outside the doorway.

Finance gets on her cell phone, takes a deep breath, and
starts shouting and cursing.

Corporate smiles and walks away.

INT. BOARDROOM - DAY

                    CORPORATE
          Tell me we're ready.
                    SUPPLY
          We're good to go.

                    CORPORATE
          #3?

                    TRANSPORT
          Ready when you are.

                    CORPORATE
          #4?

                    FINANCE
          Everything's set.

Corporate gives Science a hard look.

                    SCIENCE
          We've been waiting on *you*.

Corporate grins.

                    CORPORATE
          Yeah right. #6.

                    ENGINEERING
          Paint that shit gold.

Corporate snorts.

                    CORPORATE
           Do it, #5.

EXT. FIELD - DAY

Fossil fuel power stations across the United States
explode.

EXT - DAY

The sun rises.

Sunshine glints on multiple football field-sized solar
arrays.

The sun sets.

Patches of wind turbines rotate in other areas.

Waves crash over rotating machinery.

The sun rises.

Sunshine glints on buildings, on trains, on ships, on
cars, on buses, on planes, on space craft.

FADE OUT
THE END

Screenplay 12

Roads to Mexico

CAST OF CHARACTERS

Delia Oliver - Black American, mid 30s, female

Delores Oliver - Black American, late 30s, female

Interviewer/Officer/El Presidente - Mexican, mid 40s, male

Soldier (voice) - Mexican, male

Detainee #1 (voice)

Detainee #2 (voice)

TIME
Near future.

FADE IN

INT. QUERÉTARO:HACIENDA:2029 - DAY

We see DELIA over the INTERVIEWER's shoulder, both seated.

            DELIA
        Where should I begin?

            INTERVIEWER
        Tell   me   what   led   you   to
        Mexico.

Delia laughs aloud.

            DELIA
        All roads led to Mexico. You
        know this.

            INTERVIEWER
        Still, I want to hear your
        story.

            DELIA
        Very well.

EXT. TEXAS-MEXICO BORDER:DETENTION CAMP:2023 - DAY

Delia and DELORES wait in a line.

            DELORES
        Will it be okay?

            DELIA
        Someone told me they they turn
        people away if they don't like
        the answers you give them.

            DELORES
        We need to rest. We need
        baths.

                    DELIA
          And food and water, I know.
          But, we have to do whatever it
          takes to get over the border.
          Otherwise...

                    DELORES
          We can't go back, Delia.
          They'll kill us, just like
          Dad.

                    DELIA
          Delores, I know. Just let me
          do the talking, okay? Shhh.

An OFFICER seated at a table, wearing sunglasses, gestures
the two women forward.

                    OFFICER (in Spanish)
          ¡Avanzen! ¿Quienes son Uds.?

                    DELIA
          Delia Oliver.

                    OFFICER
          ¿Y ella?

                    DELIA
          Es mi hermana. Delores Oliver.

                    OFFICER
          ¿Marido y niños?

                    DELIA
          No tengo ni.

                    OFFICER
          ¿Y ella?

                    DELIA
          Ni tampoco ella.

The Officer looks at Delores with speculation and takes more notes.

Delia appears worried.

> OFFICER
> ¿Dónde están sus parientes?

Delia looks down and swallows.

> DELIA
> Están muertos.

The Officer nods and makes a note.

> OFFICER
> ¿Cuántos años tiene Ud.?

Delia hesitates.

> OFFICER
> ¡Respóndeme!

> DELIA (uncertainly)
> Treinta y tres.

The Officer points at Delores.

> DELIA
> Treinta y siete.

Delia bites her lip.

> DELORES
> Delia, what did he...

> OFFICER (yelling)
> ¡Fuera de aquí!

The Officer waves Delores away as if he wonders why Delores is so stupid.

Another officer's volt gun points Delores to one side.

Delia shakes her head, pleadingly.

                  OFFICER
      Usted habla español.

                  DELIA
   Si.

The Officer holds his hand out to the side.

Someone hands the Officer a sheaf of papers.

He reads a little and nods his head, slightly.

                  OFFICER
   ¿Y   asistió   usted   a   la
   universidad?

                  DELIA
   Si.

                  OFFICER
   ¿Y trabajó Ud.?

                  DELIA
   Al principio, con permiso.

                  OFFICER
   ¿Qué tipo del empleo?

Delia swallows.

                  DELIA
   Investigación.

                  OFFICER
   ¿Que tipo de investigación?

                  DELIA
   In- investigación electrónica.

The Officer freezes. He sits back in his chair for a long
moment.

                    OFFICER
               Hay dos.

Delia glances over to see Delores looking back at her
anxiously.

She nods at the Officer.

                    OFFICER
               Una va a cruzar al México.

                    DELIA
               ¿Una? What?

                    OFFICER
               Tenemos límites de población.
               La otra volverá.

                    DELIA
               No. Please!

The Officer slams his hand on the table.

                    OFFICER
               ¡Háblame en español! Ud está
               en México.

                    DELORES
               Delia, what's happening?

The Officer points a volt gun at Delia.

                    DELORES
               No!

Keeping his gun and attention on Delia, the Officer points
a finger at Delores.

                    OFFICER
               ¡No me hablas!

                    DELIA
               Delores, don't talk.

The Officer looks from Delia to Delores.

Delia shakes her head at Delores.

>   DELIA
> Lo siento. Por favor. Lo
> siento mucho. ¿No hay nada que
> pueda Ud. hacer? Somos la
> única familia que tenemos. Nos
> gustaría permanecer juntos si
> pudiéramos.

>   OFFICER
> ¡Una de ustedes volverá!
> (points at Delores) ¡Dile a
> ella lo mismo ahora!

Delia flinches back, closes her eyes, and nods her head.

She walks to Delores who hugs her.

>   DELORES
> What's happening, Delia? What
> did he say?

Delia bursts into tears unable to speak.

>   OFFICER (shouting)
> ¡Darse prisa!

>   DELIA
> They have population limits.
> He said only one of us could
> cross. The other has to
> return.

Delores's voices rises in outrage.

The officer slams his fist on the table.

>   OFFICER
> ¡Una entrará México o ninguna
> entrará México!

Delia whispers the translation.

                    DELORES
          I'll go back.

Delia and Delores argue and whisper back and forth.

                    OFFICER
          ¡Ya!

                    DELIA
          Quiet, Delores. Do as I say.
          If you argue he'll return us
          both to North American
          authorities.

Delores stares at Delia, then nods.

Delia returns to the seated Officer.

                    OFFICER
          Una volverá.

                    DELIA
          Una (pause) volverá.

                    OFFICER
          ¿Y entonces?

Delia looks at the Officer with hatred. The Officer seems
amused.

                    OFFICER
          ¿Usted?

Staring into Delia's face, the Officer barks rapid orders.

He flicks a dismissive hand at Delores.

                    OFFICER
          Ella estará a salvo.

                    DELORES (wailing)
          Delia. Oh my, God. Wait!
          Delia!

Delia refuses to look at Delores.

She stares into the Officer's eyes.

A soldier's arms shove Delores into a truck.

Delia turns to look, then turns back to the Officer.

                    DELIA
          What are you doing? I said *I*
          would go back! (pointing) You
          said she would be safe!

The Officer doesn't answer.

                    DELIA (lowering voice)
          Yo sé que usted todavía tiene
          honor.

Delia stares at the Officer a long moment, then turns her
back to watch the truck disappear into a cloud of dust.

                    DELIA (whispering)
          I said that *I* would go back.

Delia trembles. Tears fill her eyes.

She stands dazed and silent.

The Officer finishes stamping papers. He shuffles the
papers around as if nothing important happened.

He doesn't look at Delia when he orders...

                    OFFICER
          Llévela   al   centro   de
          detención.

Arms grip Delia's elbows and snatch her away.

INT. QUERÉTARO:HACIENDA:2029 - DAY

          INTERVIEWER
Was that the worst moment?

          DELIA
I don't like to talk about
it.
          INTERVIEWER
No, you don't.

          DELIA
That was then. This is now.

          INTERVIEWER
Am I upsetting you?

          DELIA
No. Just the memory of it all
coming back. I closed that
door.

          INTERVIEWER
Yes. I'm sorry. Do you wish
to continue?

          DELIA
We've come this far. May as
well go all the way. (deep
breath) Like I said, the
corporations changed the bot
programming from labor to law
enforcement. The next step,
obviously, was combat.

EXT. TEXAS-MEXICO BORDER:DETENTION CAMP:2023 - DAY

Delia sits on a concrete block.

She looks through the fence at dusty nothingness.

                    DETAINEE #1 (voice)
          They say bots are on the march
          through Texas.

                    DETAINEE #2 (voice)
          How far away?

                    DETAINEE #1 (voice)
          I heard two days from the
          East, West, and North.

                    DETAINEE #2 (voice)
          Wonder what's gonna happen
          when the tin cans show up?

                    DETAINEE #1 (voice)
          I'm gonna jump this fence,
          that's what.

                    DETAINEE #2 (voice)
          With all those guns?

                    DETAINEE #1 (voice)
          The guns won't be pointed at
          us, will they?

Three shadows loomed past over Delia.

                    SOLDIER (voice)
          Delia Oliver.

                    DELIA
          Yes.

                    SOLDIER (voice)
          Come with us.

EXT. TEXAS-MEXICO BORDER:DETENTION CAMP:2023 - DAY

Delia is shoved from behind into a nondescript office.

The Officer sits behind a desk.

A volt rifle guards Delia from behind.

          OFFICER
Delia Oliver.

          DELIA
Sí.

          OFFICER
Su hermana sigue bajo el
control total del ejército
mexicano, como lo hace usted.
Contesta con la verdad para
que ella pueda seguir
viviendo.

Delia blinks her eyes.

          DELIA
Claro. De acuerdo.

The Officer flips through her file reading parts here and
there.

He glances up at Delia now and then as if to compare her
disheveled appearance with her file.

He places her file on the desk.

          OFFICER
Cuando le pregunté, usted
retuvo información de mí.

          DELIA
Contesté todas las preguntas.

          OFFICER
Se pregunté dónde trabajó.

Delia frowns.

                    DELIA
          Usted me preguntó qué tipo de
          trabajo   que   hacía.   Dije
          investigación   electrónica. Es
          la verdad.

The Officer smolders. He slams his fist on the desk.

                    OFFICER
          ¡No!   Usted   trabajó   para
          Robocorp!

                    DELIA
          Si. Yo hice la investigación
          electrónica para Robocorp. Me
          despidieron   hace   dos   años.
          Pero   nunca   me   preguntó
          ¿dónde? Acabas de preguntar
          ¿qué? Le dije la verdad que
          usted me pidió.

Delia hears the slightest shuffle behind her.

The volt gun guarding her shifts position.

                    OFFICER
          Me desobedece ... aunque sea
          una   vez   más   ...   y   ella
          morirá. Usted se quedará con
          vida   para   considerar   su
          decisión por el resto de sus
          días miserables.

                    DELIA
          Okay! Okay. Please,   don't.
          Just... Dime lo que quiere
          saber.

                    OFFICER
          ¡Dime la verdad!

The Officer slams his fist on the desk.

OFFICER
La verdad o ella muere. Y
Ud. habrá matadola.

Delia's shoulders slump.

DELIA
Entonces, ¿En qué puedo
ayudarle?

The Officer leans back in his chair and nods approval.

The Officer stands up and walks around his desk to a map
of North and South America on the wall.

The Officer gives Delia a long look.

OFFICER
Los Yankees quieren mantener
Tejas. No lo harán, claro,
porque México quiere volver a
tomar toda la mitad inferior
de los Estados Unidos,
incluyendo California, Utah,
Colorado, Arizona, Nuevo
México, Oklahoma, Florida,
Louisiana. Además, toda la
costa del Golfo y de la costa
del Atlántico sur. (pause) y
Tejas.

Delia shifts, uneasy.

                    OFFICER
          Los Estados Unidos tiene
          armas nucleares. Pero México
          comparte una frontera, la
          tierra, el agua y el aire.
          Armas nucleares en México
          ensuciaría su propio patio
          trasero. Los Estados Unidos
          tienen sus aliados. Pero,
          Señorita Delia, usted se
          sorprenderá de lo que haría
          la gente para propiedad.
          (laughs) Como lo dicen,
          ¡Colocación!   ¡Colocación!
          ¡Colocación!

The Officer snaps down a second map with a dramatic
flourish.

                    OFFICER
          ¿Qué haría a Rusia por Alaska
          y el petróleo de Alaska? ¿Qué
          se parece, Señorita?

He looks with expectation at Delia.

                    DELIA
          I don't want to know anymore.
          Don't tell me anything else.

                    OFFICER
          Todo lo México se puede pedir.
          México pidió a Rusia a mirar
          hacia otro lado, sólo por un
          tiempo, y luego plantar una
          bandera en Juneau.

The Officer flicks his fingers towards the Pacific Ocean
on the map.

                    OFFICER
          Japón ha soñado durante mucho
          tiempo   de   Hawai   y   los
          territorios   del   Pacífico.
          México   hará   realidad   ese
          sueño.   Pero   lo   más
          maquiavélico de todos (pause)
          Canada ha acordado adoptar los
          Grandes   Lagos,   Nueva
          Inglaterra, el Atlántico norte
          y el noroeste del Pacífico de
          nuestras manos. Ah, querido
          Canada.

The Officer laughs.

                    OFFICER
          Everything and everyone has
          its   price.   Including   you,
          Señorita Delia.

Delia frowns without speaking.

                    OFFICER
          It's   true,   isn't   it?
          (shrugging) América del Sur y
          el Caribe van a esperar para
          ver   lo   que   logra   México.
          Mientras   tanto,   van   a
          proporcionar   suministros,
          armas y soldados para mantener
          a Europa de distancia. Y, por
          supuesto, México ha solicitado
          que   los   mexicano-americanos
          que quedan al norte de la
          frontera   luchen   donde   se
          encuentren para Mexico.

The Officer stands in Delia's face.

                    OFFICER
          We are going to win, Señorita.

                    DELIA
          Sí. Es obvio, ¿no?

The Officer walks behind the desk.

He takes his time stacking the papers in her file
together.

                    OFFICER
          El control del ejército bot
          sigue siendo un obstáculo.

The Officer leans back in his chair and meets Delia's
gaze.

After an awkward silence...

                    DELIA
          Soy leal a la nación que
          alberga mi única familia
          restante.

                    OFFICER
          ¿Y entonces?

The Officer shrugs and places his hand on top of her file,
tapping it with his fingertips, triggering another long
silence.
                    DELIA
          La división de seguridad en
          Robocorp construyó una puerta
          de entrada a la red bot. Es
          un mecanismo de seguridad,
          para evitar que la tecnología
          se   expanda   demasiado
          rápidamente o ser adquirida
          por   (pause)   intereses
          externos.

The Officer puts her file into a folder, and then places
the folder into the top right drawer of the desk.

                    OFFICER
          Llévala subterráneo.

INT. QUERÉTARO:HACIENDA:2029 - DAY

                    INTERVIEWER
          That's quite a story.

                    DELIA
          Long story short.

                    INTERVIEWER
          Not very romantic.

                    DELIA
          No. Not very. Is it?

Long pause.

                    INTERVIEWER
          So underground…

                    DELIA
          Well, there's more than that.

INT. TEXAS-MEXICO BORDER:DETENTION CAMP:2043 - DAY

On her way underground, Delia overhears a loudspeaker.

                    OFFICER (voice)
          Usted será entrenado en las
          armas voltios y otras armas.
          La   deserción   o   la
          insubordinación significa que
          su ejecución inmediata por
          parte del Ejército Mexicano.
          Aquellos que tratan de evadir
          el   Ejército   Mexicano   será
          abandonado a los robots que ya
          han demostrado su falta de
          simpatía por la vida humana.

Underground, Delia works with the electronic specialists to defeat the computer codes that program the bots.

                    OFFICER
          Veinticuatro horas.

Delia toils over a computer monitor.

She sleeps in the fetal position.

Over Delia's shoulder, the Officer bores two holes into Delia's back with his eyes.

Delia continues her efforts at the computer.

She shuts down the bot army and everyone cheers.

INT. QUERÉTARO:HACIENDA:2023 - DAY

                    INTERVIEWER
          You   must   have   made   the
          Officer happy.

                    DELIA (coldly)
          So it would seem.

The Interviewer shifts in his chair.

                    DELIA
          Immigrants from South America
          streamed into Lower and Upper
          Mexico.   Mexico,   Canada,
          Japan, and Russia restricted
          the   White   population   to
          Montana,   Wyoming,   Nebraska,
          Kansas,   North   Dakota,   South
          Dakota,   Iowa   reservations.
          And   today,   bots   and   remote
          sentries   still   patrol   the
          inside   perimeters   of   the
          reservations and the borders
          of the surrounding states.

INT. MEXICO:DETENTION CENTER:2025 - DAY

          OFFICER
Ha servido bien México durante
dos años. Ha completado su
deber, Señorita. Usted es
libre de irse.

          DELIA
Go where? Do what?

          OFFICER
Tu hermana te espera.

          DELIA
You know where she is?

          OFFICER
Siempre lo he sabido.

          DELIA
Pero me preguntaba por tanto
tiempo. Ni siquiera sabía si
estaba viva. Ud. nunca me
dició...

          OFFICER
Ella está a salvo. Te llevaré
con ella.

          DELIA (surprised)
¿Tú?

The Officer raises his eyebrows in challenge.

          OFFICER
Salimos de Querétaro mañana
en la mañana.

Delia backs slowly to the door as if she doesn't believe
him.

The Officer draws himself up.

                    OFFICER
          Tengo   el   honor,   Señorita
          Oliver.

INT. QUERÉTARO:HACIENDA:2029 - DAY

                    INTERVIEWER
          I'm starting to see.

                    DELIA
          Do you?

INT/EXT. QUERÉTARO:ROAD:2025 - DAY

The Officer drives Delia in the truck.

                    DELIA
          Are you happy with all that
          you've accomplished?

                    OFFICER
          The world is better. A better
          world makes better people.

                    DELIA
          The   bots,   you're   satisfied
          with their direction?

                    OFFICER (sighing)
          Yes, Señorita Delia, I'm
          extremely satisfied. Las
          funciones de riesgo
          realizadas por los robots con
          su programación salva vidas
          humanas. Desde luego tomaron
          suficientes vidas durante la
          guerra. En unos diez años,
          los residuos nucleares, los
          océanos y los lagos deben
          proporcionar recursos limpios
          una vez más. Silicio minera
          de los paneles solares es
          antes de lo previsto. So,
          yes, I am satisfied. Thank
          you.

                    DELIA
          And the replants?

                    OFFICER
          América Central y del Sur han
          mostrado su gratitud en
          diversas formas en que la
          reposición de sus selvas.

Delia looks out the window at the Mexican landscape
rushing past.

                    DELIA
          Why are *you* taking me to my
          sister?

                    OFFICER
          Would you rather stay at the
          detention camp?

                    DELIA
          Why not one of your
          soldiers?

The Officer's eyes flick Delia's way.

                    OFFICER
          You   wonder   if   you   will
          actually   reach   your
          destination.

                    DELIA
          Will I?

                    OFFICER
          As I said before, you're
          joining your sister.

Delia closes her eyes wearily.

She wakes as the truck bumps along a dust road that led to
a hacienda.

EXT. QUERÉTARO:HACIENDA:2025 - DAY

Delores walks out of the front door, pregnant, using a
remote to guide a stroller with another child.

                    DELORES
          Delia!

                    DELIA
          Delores!

The   sisters   embrace   and   Delores   speaks   over   Delia's
shoulder.

                    DELORES
          Hermano, ¡Gracias para traerla
          a casa!

                    DELIA (confused)
          Hermano? Delores, you speak
          Spanish now?

The Officer returns Delia's gaze without expression.

                    DELIA
               Hermano?

Mexican women exit the house this time and surround the
Officer with hugs and kisses.

Delia looks disoriented.

                    DELIA (whispering)
               Brother?

Delores and the women rush back inside chattering about
the meal they'll prepare for Delia and The Officer.

                    OFFICER
               Hice lo que tenía que hacer
               por México. Como lo hiciste.
               Ahora eres libre, Delia. Pero
               creo que (pause) tu hermana
               le gustaría quedarse aquí.

The Officer walks away from the wounded look in Delia's
eyes.

Delia, after a look at arid landscape, slowly follows him
inside.

EXT. QUERÉTARO:HACIENDA:2025 - DAY

Delia sits with Delores on the bed in a spare room.

                    DELORES
               They brought me to his house.
               His family took care of me.
               He visited now and then to
               tell us how you helped the
               cause. See?

Delores turns on a hologram of Delia working underground
at the detention camp.

                    DELORES
          I wasn't happy that you had to
          work for both of us and so far
          away, but, I realized worse
          things could have happened.
          I've been happy here.

Delores took Delia's hand turning her own to show a
wedding band.

                    DELIA (shocked)
          You're married?

Delia puts her head in her hands to slow the dizziness.

                    DELIA
          Oh my God. What has happened
          here?

Delores puts an arm around Delia.

                    DELORES
          I fell in love, Delia.

                    DELIA
          In love with...

                    DELORES
          I know it's a lot to take in
          all at once. But I made a new
          life. Everyone who left the
          States made new lives.

                    DELIA
          I had no idea of any of this.
          But to *him*? After the way he
          treated us at the border?

Delores gives Delia a strange look and shakes her head.

                    DELORES
          No, Delia. I married his
          brother. Miguel. You'll meet
          him soon.

                    DELIA
          Oh. His brother, Miguel.

                    DELORES
          With one-and-a-half children.

Delia still looks stunned.

                    DELORES
          I asked for permission to
          communicate with you but he
          wouldn't allow it. He assured
          us that you were safe. Were
          you okay? No one…

                    DELIA
          No. I… no one ever bothered
          me. The soldiers, the other
          detainees… they always kept
          their distance.

                    DELORES
          He kept you safe for two
          years.

Delia looked down at her own hands clasped together.

                    DELIA
          I guess.

                    DELORES (smiling)
          Maybe there's a reason.

                    DELIA
          He didn't lie to me, but
          he...

                    DELORES
          But what?

Delia shakes her head.

                    DELORES (laughing)
          You looked so relieved when
          you realized I was talking
          about his brother.

Delores hugs Delia.

                    DELORES
          Shower and lay down, Delia.
          There's an hour until dinner.
          The men will be there and
          then we can all talk about
          things.

Delia stands in the doorway of the living room.

Delores calls Delia into the room.

Delia locks eyes with The Officer.

The Officer rises to stand beside her.

INT. QUERÉTARO:HACIENDA:2029 - DAY

                    DELIA
          And so, I received an offer of
          marriage.

                    INTERVIEWER
          And you said…

                    DELIA
          I said the only thing left to
          say.

                    INTERVIEWER
          Did you love him?

INT. QUERÉTARO:HACIENDA:2025 - DAY

Delia places her hand into the Officer's hand.

INT. QUERÉTARO:HACIENDA:2029 - DAY

                    DELIA
          All roads led to Mexico.

                    INTERVIEWER
          But, did you love him? Even
          after all he put you through?

Delia sighs and goes to stand at the window.

                    INTERVIEWER
          Do you think you would be
          where you are now if…

Delia closes her eyes.

                    DELIA
          I told you that all roads led
          to Mexico.

                    INTERVIEWER
          Yes. You told me that.

                    DELIA
          The real truth is, all roads
          led me home. His heart is my
          home. My heart is his home...
          but only if he wishes it. I
          can't... (firm voice) We're
          done here.

The Interviewer stands up.

                    INTERVIEWER
          This is good for El Presidente
          to know.

                    DELIA
          Well now he knows!

Delia starts to cry.

                    INTERVIEWER
          Now that you've said it out loud,
          mi esposa.

The Interviewer stands in full military regalia.

El Presidente kisses Delia with passion.

                    EL PRESIDENTE
          Now that you finally love me
          and trust me the way I love
          and trust you. Now that you
          forgive me, we are both home.

El Presidente kisses Delia again.

FADE OUT
THE END

About the Author

Lee McQueen has a Master of Library Science from State University of New York at Buffalo, a Bachelor of Arts from Xavier University of Louisiana, and coursework in public affairs at the University of Texas at Austin.

She has been both a librarian and a bookstore owner. Now editor and publisher at McQueen Press, she also takes on writing and research assignments.

Projects with McQueen Press include the novels *Kenzi, Celara Sun, Windrunner*; the poetry collection *Things I Forgot to Tell You*; the screenplays *SUDAN: The Lion of Truth* and Octavia Butler's *Kindred*; the non-fiction reference *Writer in the Library! 41 Writers Reveal How They Use Libraries to Develop Their Skill, Craft & Careers*; the travel memoir *Road Romance: Tales from the Book Tour*, and original greeting card designs.

Visit http://mcqueenpress.wordpress.com for more information.

Acknowledgements

Thank you, to all the folks and organizations who made it possible for me to finish this book of screenplays. In particular, Homer McQueen, Ora McQueen, Kathy and David Gemperle, Chicago Transit Authority, Truman College, Chicago Public Library, Chicago Cultural Center, Chicago Independent Artists Network, St. Thomas of Canterbury, Our Lady of Lourdes, Sarah's Circle, and Cornerstone Outreach. Somehow, despite the odds, we did it!

McQueen Press Publications

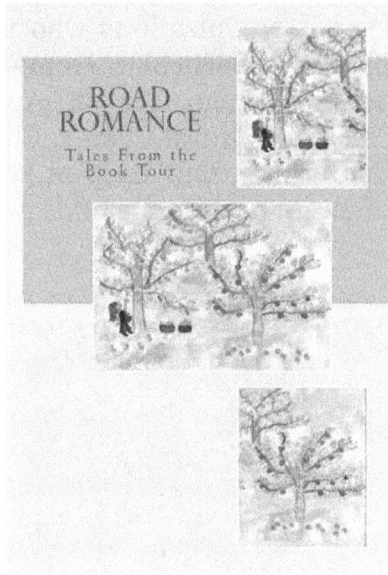

Travel Memoir
ISBN-13: 978-0979851568
2013

In 2012, Lee McQueen traveled from Colorado through Kansas, Oklahoma, Arkansas, Tennessee, Mississippi, Alabama, Georgia, Missouri, Illinois, Iowa, Nebraska, and then back to Colorado to promote her latest romance novel.

From Beale Street to Route 66 to the Great River Road, to Colfax Avenue--in the spirit of Jack Kerouac and Johnny Appleseed--she fell in love with the road.

This collection of journal entries, blog postings, narration in retrospect, and watercolors reveals surprises on Lee's journey through Middle America.

Lee McQueen

Windrunner

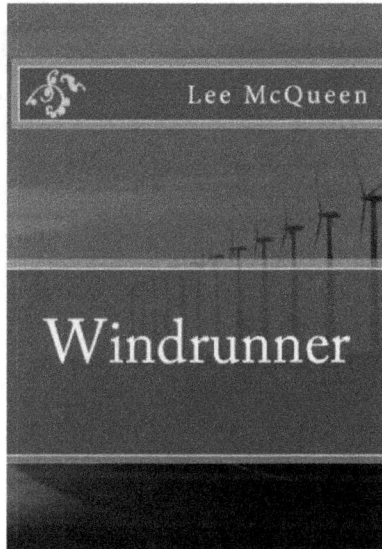

Suspense/Romance Novel
ISBN-13: 978-0979851575
2012

A cross-country chase carries Tolly Henry and Scott Windrunner on an adventure from Midwestern rolling prairies to southwestern Rocky Mountains.

Roadside motels, truckstops, corn silos, and windmills guide Scott's whirlwind rundown of Tolly amid echoes of past military service, domestic violence, and post-traumatic stress.

Only if our two heroes join together to defeat the corrupt forces that pit them against each other will Scott and Tolly have a second chance to reclaim their lives and love for each other.

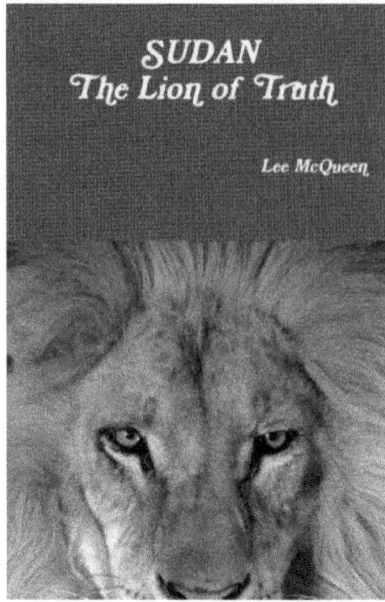

Action/Adventure Screenplay
ISBN-13: 978-0979851599
2nd ed.
2011

On a Christian mission to redeem slaves in Sudan, a reformed female gang member Davey is kidnapped and sold into slavery herself. She uses her former street experiences and talent for leadership to convince the other slaves to break free and flee to the Ethiopian border. Everything Davey has ever learned will save her life.

Join Davey's journey as she realizes that it's not where you're from, but where you're going that matters. Set in Dallas, Khartoum, Atbarah, and Kassala.

While the first edition of *The Angel and the Lion* was 8 ½ x 11, the second edition, titled *SUDAN: The Lion of Truth* has been adjusted to traditional trade paperback size, 6 x 9 for easier distribution. Besides the new cover, while there have been additions and deletions to the front and back matter and minor punctuation edits to the short story, the text of the actual screenplay remains unchanged.

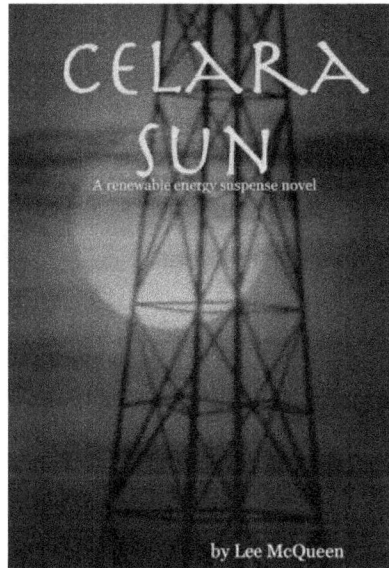

Suspense/Drama Novel
ISBN-13: 978-0979851582
2010

As *Dallas* and *Dynasty* showcased the wealth, sex, intrigue, and power that drove the oil industry, so *Celara Sun* reveals the tumultuous world behind solar and wind.

Martina Butler matches Alexander King step-for-step in a battle of wills to control Lake City's solar and wind energy markets. "Clean energy is a dirty business," and "You have to go green to get green," sum up Alex's philosophy towards power.

During the green revolution, the players realize that life moves forward, never backward—and it certainly doesn't stand still.

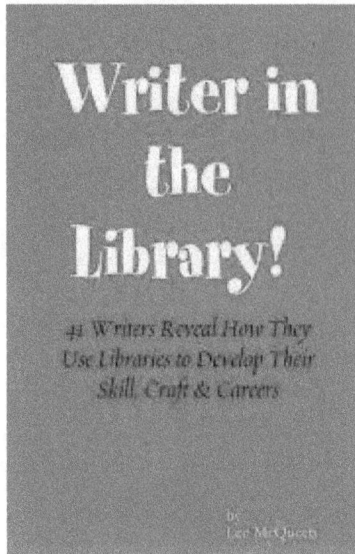

Non-fiction/Reference
ISBN-13: 978-0979851544
2008

This non-fiction reference work collects the interviews and submissions of fiction and non-fiction writers who discuss the impact of libraries on their career development. Numerous transcripts, photos, biographies, library quotations, footnotes, a glossary, and an index present the information as a teaching tool for the reader.

The contributors cross gender, race, political, philosophical, cultural, subject, and genre lines. Each had something significant to share about the importance of the library to the writer.

Writer in the Library! has been added to many fine collections such as Ames Public Library, Chicago Public Library, Drake University, Grand View University, Illinois State Library, Los Angeles Public Library, University of Chicago, Iowa State University, Loras College, Allen Public Library, University of Iowa, Iowa City Public Library, University of Nevada, University of Northern Iowa Library, West Des Moines Public Library, Winterset Public Library, Woodward Public Library, Xavier University of Louisiana, etc.

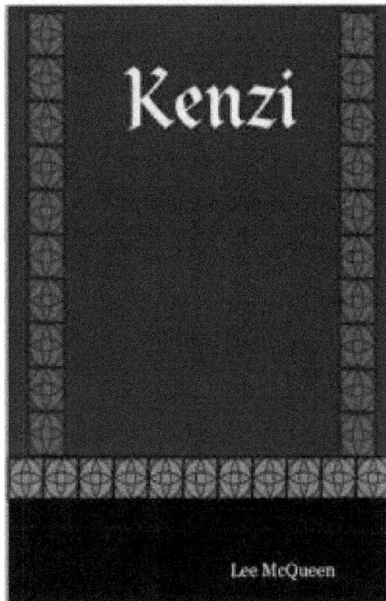

Kenzi

Lee McQueen

Romance/Family Drama Novel
ISBN-13: 978-0979851520
2007

Kenzi, an intelligent, sensitive woman living in small-town Texas, feels alienated from the person she knows she should be and would be if only she truly believed it possible.

If Kenzi finds the ability to forgive her own mistakes and the mistakes of others, she may have a chance to meet her destiny head-on.

Things I
Forgot to
Tell You

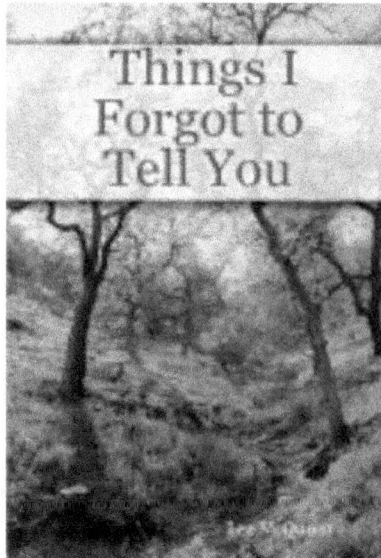

Poetry Collection
ISBN 978-0-978515-3-7
2007
2nd ed.
Out of Print

Poems speak on uncertainty, sadness, despair, guilt, anger, frustration, love, hope, forgiveness, happiness, joy, and spirituality.

Poetry is interactive.

The reader or listener meets the author or speaker halfway and fills the poem with their own reality and expectations.

A lot like life and diamonds, poetry reflects back an image that depends on where one stands in relation to the expressions.

Short Story Collection
ISBN-13: 978-0979851506
2006

Fourteen short stories describe inner turmoil that drives change.

Especially when the characters who inhabit the stories step outside the ordinary for a moment in time.

And so, there remains the Imaginarium, where Dreamers know when to take a chance and Heroes know when to make a stand.

Because refusing to make a choice is a choice.

And sometimes, the least of all has the greatest ability to influence the future of the world.

McQueen Greetings

Original Watercolor Designs by Lee McQueen

Available on Greeting Cards and Other Merchandise

http://www.cafepress.com/mcqueenpress

McQueen Press Merchandise

These Gift Ideas and More

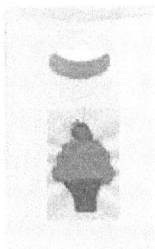

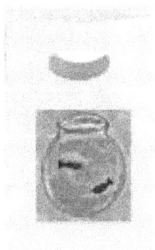

Available at

http://www.cafepress.com/mcqueenpress

The Ship of Fools

The Seeker
Went out
But never returned
So they sent
Another one

This ship of fools
Followed The Seeker
And found Cruel World
Not foreign
Alien

The warning beacon cried
Fear, pain, death
Unspeakable
Unexplainable
Inhuman

A world where
Humans are the pets
Cattle
Product
Food

Arrogant on Earth
Subjugated on
Cruel World
Reduced to
Humiliation

The caste system
The aliens created
Abominable
Indescribable
Suicidal

The Seeker
Is gone
Of the ship of fools
Only two remain
Alive

But not alive
Comatose
Male and female
Locked together
Tethered

Forced to
Reproduce like
Beasts
For the aliens
Cattle

Years go by
The humans
Reproduce and
Provide more humans
For alien harvest

Before the slaughter
Before the cages
The ship of fools
Sent another beacon
To warn Earth

About the cages
Locked into place
Like beasts
Forced to rape
Each other

Mothers and sons
Fathers and daughters
Sisters and brothers
The aliens
Did not care

They feed the humans
Breed the humans
Harvest the humans
Eat the humans
Wear the humans

Two humans
Remain in stasis
Alive
But not Alive
Aware

Screaming
Insanity
Praying for
Heart attacks
Now comatose

Milk, Blood, Semen
Urine, Saliva, Skin
The aliens
Find uses
For everything

The alien race
Will increase
Their herd of
Earth beasts and
Earth meat

But will it ever
Be enough?
Because of The Seeker
And the Ship of Fools
The aliens know Earth

Cruel World
They like us
They want us
They want more
They will find us

www.ingramcontent.com/pod-product-compliance
Lightning Source LLC
Chambersburg PA
CBHW081323090426

42737CB00017B/3009